Adam Gurowski

The History of Slavery

Madison & Adams Press 2019

Charles A. Eastman
CHARLES EASTMAN Premium Collection: Indian Boyhood, Indian
Heroes and Great Chieftains, The Soul of the Indian & From the Deep
Woods to Civilization

Charles Oman
The History of Byzantine Empire

John Dixon Long
Pictures of Slavery in Church and State

Theodore Roosevelt
Theodore Roosevelt's Letters to His Children

U.S. Army Center of Military History, Robert W. Coakley
The American Revolution (Vol. 1-3)

Charles Carleton Coffin
Old Times in the Colonies (Illustrated Edition)

Charles Carleton Coffin
The Story of Liberty & Old Times in the Colonies (Illustrated Edition)

Beckwith West
Experience of a Confederate States Prisoner

Sara Agnes Rice Pryor
The Birth of the Nation (Illustrated Edition)

Charles Carleton Coffin
Daughters of the Revolution and Their Times (Illustrated Edition)

Adam Gurowski
The History of Slavery

Madison & Adams Press, 2019
Contact: info@madisonadamspress.com

ISBN 978-80-273-3443-8

This is a publication of Madison & Adams Press. Our production consists of thoroughly prepared educational & informative editions: Advice & How-To Books, Encyclopedias, Law Anthologies, Declassified Documents, Legal & Criminal Files, Historical Books, Scientific & Medical Publications, Technical Handbooks and Manuals. All our publications are meticulously edited and formatted to the highest digital standard. The main goal of Madison & Adams Press is to make all informative books and records accessible to everyone in a high quality digital and print form.

Contents

Introduction   11

I. Egyptians   14

II. Phœnicians   19

III. Libyans   22

IV. Carthaginians   24

V. Hebrews, or Beni-Israel   25

VI. Nabatheans   34

VII. Assyrians and Babylonians   36

VIII. Medes and Persians   38

IX. Aryas—Hindus   40

X. Chinese   43

XI. Greeks   46

XII. Romans—The Republicans   55

XIII. Romans—Political Slaves   63

XIV. Christianity: Its Churches and Creeds   69

XV. Gauls   72

XVI. Germans   75

XVII. Longobards—Italians   81

XVIII. Franks—French   84

XIX. Britons, Anglo-Saxons, English.   89

XX. Slavi, Slavonians, Slaves, Russians   93

XXI. Conclusion   99

Footnotes   103

Introduction

For the first time in the annals of humanity, domestic slavery, or the system of chattelhood and traffic in man, is erected into a religious, social and political creed. This new creed has its thaumaturgus, its temples, its altars, its worship, its divines, its theology, its fanatical devotees; it has its moralists, its savants and sentimentalists, its statesmen and its publicists. The articles of this new faith are preached and confessed by senators and representatives in the highest councils of the American people, as well as in the legislatures of the respective States; they are boldly proclaimed by the press, and by platform orators and public missionaries; in a word, this new faith over-shadows the whole religious, social, intellectual, political and economical existence of a large portion of the Republic.

The less fervent disciples consider domestic slavery as an eminently practical matter, and regard those of an opposite opinion as abstruse theorizers; and history is called in and ransacked for the purpose of justifying the present by the past.

Well: history contains *all* the evidences-multifarious and decisive.

It is asserted that domestic slavery has always been a constructive social element: history shows that it has always been destructive. History authoritatively establishes the fact that slavery is the most corroding social disease, and one, too, which acts most fatally on the slaveholding element in a community.

Not disease, but health, is the normal condition of man's physical organism: not oppression but freedom is the normal condition of human society. The laws of history are as absolute as the laws of nature or the laws of hygiene. As an individual cannot with impunity violate hygienic law-as nature *always* avenges every departure from her eternal order: so nations and communities cannot safely deviate from the laws of history, still less violate them with impunity. History positively demonstrates that slavery is not one of the natural laws of the human race, any more than disorders and monstrosities are normal conditions of the human body.

History demonstrates that slavery is not coeval with, nor inherent in, human society, but is the offspring of social derangement and decay. The healthiest physical organism may, under certain conditions, develop from within, or receive by infection from without, diseases which are coeval, so to speak, with the creation, and which hover perpetually over animal life. The disease, too, may be acute or chronic, according to the conditions or predispositions of the organism. History teaches that domestic slavery may, at times, affect the healthiest social organism, and be developed, like other social disorders and crimes, so to speak, in the very womb of the nation. As the tendency of vigorous health is to prevent physical derangements and diseases, so the tendency of society in its most elevated conception is to prevent, to limit, to neutralize, if not wholly to extirpate, all social disorders. Not depravity and disease, but purity and virtue, are the normal condition of the individual: not oppression but freedom is the normal condition of society.

Some investigators and philosophers discover an identity between the progressive development of the human body and the various stages of human society-beginning with the embryonic condition of both. More than one striking analogy certainly exists between physiological and pathological laws, and the moral and social principles which ought to be observed by man both as an individual, and in the aggregate called society. Thus some of the pathologic axioms established by Rokitansky[1] (the greatest of living pathologists) are equally sustained by the history of nations.

> "No formation is incapable of becoming diseased in one or more ways. Several anomalies coexisting in an organ commonly stand to each other in the relation of cause and effect. Thus, deviation in texture determines deviation in size, in form."

The following pages will demonstrate that nations and communities may become diseased in many ways; and that in proportion as their social textures deviate from the normal, do they become more and more deformed and demoralized.

"All anomalies of organization involving any anatomical change manifest themselves as deviations in the quantity or quality of organic creation, or else as a mechanical separation of continuity. They are reducible to irregular number, size, form, continuity, and contents."

Oppressions, tyrannies, domestic slavery, chattelhood, are so many mechanical separations of continuity, which in the social organic creation is liberty.

"General disease engenders the most various organs and textures according to their innate, general or individual tendencies, either spontaneously or by dint of some overpowering outward impulse, a local affection which reflects the general disease in the peculiarity of its products. The general disease becomes localized, and, so to speak, represented in the topical affection."

Violence and oppression generated various and peculiar forms of servitude, until nearly all of them ended in chattelhood, which many are wont to consider as a topical affection of certain races and nations. Declining Greece and Rome in the past, Russia under our own eyes, serve as illustrations.

"A general disease not unfrequently finds in its localization a perpetual focus of derivation, with *seeming* integrity of the organism in other respects."

So nations infected with slavery, nevertheless had brilliant epochs of existence; and this "*seeming* integrity of the organism" misleads many otherwise averse to chattelhood, and makes them indifferent to its existence.

"Where several diseases coexist in an individual, they are in part *primary*, in part *secondary* and subordinate, although homologous to the former."

So many evils are the lot of human society, but almost all of them are secondary and subordinate to oppression, violence, and slavery.

"*The issue of a local disease* in health consists either in the perfect re-establishment of the normal condition, or else in partial recovery; more or fewer important residua and sequellæ of the disease not incomparable with a tolerably fair state of health, remaining entailed."

The history of the slow recovery of post-Roman Europe from domestic bondage justifies the application of this pathologic axiom to the social condition of nations.

"*Issue in death*: 1. Through exhaustion of power and of organic matter."

The history of republican, but above all, of imperial Rome, demonstrates that its decline and death were caused through the extinction of freedom, free labor, and the free yeomanry, which in every state constitutes *the power, the organic matter* of a nation.

"2. Through the suspended function of organs essential to life, through palsy, etc."

When the laboring classes are enslaved, the life of a nation is speedily palsied.

"3. Through vitiation of the blood."

What blood is to the animal organism, sound social and political principles are to society. When such principles become vitiated, the nation is on the path of decline and death.

"The worst malformation is never so anomalous as not to hear the general character of animal life, etc. Even an individual organ never departs from its normal character so completely that amid even the greatest disfigurement, this character should not be cognizable."

So often the enslaver and the slaveholding community may preserve *some* features of the normal human character, notwithstanding the "disfigurement" produced.

"The excessive development of one part determines the imperfect and retarded development of another, and the converse."

So the oligarchic development retards the growth and advancement of the laboring classes, whether the hue be white or black: it prevents or retards the culture and civilization of individuals and communities.

"Various and manifold as are the forms of monstrosity, some of them recur with such uniformity of type as to constitute a regular series."

History shows that various as are the other social monstrosities, domestic slavery always recurred with a filial uniformity of type.

"The genesis of malformation in the human body is still veiled in much obscurity despite some progress made in science."

Social *teratology*, or the science of monstrosities, easily traces the origin and genesis of domestic slavery.

A conscientious study of the records of bygone nations, as well as of the events daily witnessed during a decennium, produced the following pages. They complete what I said about slavery a few years ago.[2] As then, so now, I am almost wholly unacquainted with anti-slavery literature in any of its manifestations. I diligently sought for information in the literary and political productions of pro-slavery writers. Beside legislative enactments, political discussions, and resolutions by Congress and the legislatures of the various Slave States, and the messages of their respective governors, I read every thing that came within my reach, even sermons, heaps of "De Bow's Review" and "Fletcher's Studies on Slavery."[3] Ah!...

For years the rich resources of the Astor Library have facilitated my general studies, and the information there sought and found was enhanced by the kindest liberality experienced from Dr. Coggswell and all his assistants.

And now let History unfold her records.

I. Egyptians

AUTHORITIES:

Wilkinson, Rosellini, Lepsius, Uhlemann, Rénan, Guttschmidt, Bugsch, Birch, De Rouget, Bunsen, etc.

In the gray twilight of history, the apparition that first distinctly presents itself is *Egypt* —that land of wonders, standing on the shores of the "venerable mother the Nile." The Egyptians already form a fully-elaborated, organic social structure, nay, a powerful nation, with a rich material and intellectual civilization, when as yet the commonly accepted chronology begins to write only rudimental numbers.

It is indifferent (so far as the present investigation is concerned) whether this Egyptian culture ascended or descended the Nile-whether its cradle was Meroe, Elephantis, Syene, or Thebes-or whether it first sprang up and expanded around Memphis. So, the first conquerors of Egypt may have belonged to the Shemitic or to the Aryan stock-they may have entered from Asia by the Isthmus of Suez, or by the Straits of Bab-el-Mandeb and the Red Sea, landing first on some spot in Abyssinia or Nubia; or, perhaps, the primitive civilizers of the valley of the Nile were autochthones, who were conquered by foreign invaders. However these things may have been, Egyptian civilization and culture clearly bear the impress of indigenous development.

The founders of the Egyptian civil, social and religious polity considered agriculture as the most sacred occupation of mortals-transforming the roving savage into a civilized man. It was the divine Osiris who first taught men the art of tilling the earth, if indeed he was not its inventor. But the god forged not a fetter for the farmer, and the Egyptian plough was not desecrated by the hands of a slave.

The first rays of history reveal Egypt densely covered with farms, villages, and cities, and divided into districts (*noma*), townships, and communes-each having its distinct deity, and each most probably self-governing, or at least self-administering: all this in the earliest epoch, previous to the first dynasties of the Pharaohs, and anterior to the division of the population into castes.

The division of a population into *castes*, however destructive it may be to the growth of individuality and the highest freedom in man, is neither domestic slavery nor chattelhood. These divisions and sub-divisions originally consisted simply in training the individuals to special occupations and functions, and so educating them in special ideas; but not in making any one caste the property of any other. The gradations of caste constituted no form of chattelhood whatever.

The principal castes were the princes, or Pharaohs, the priests, the soldiers, and then the merchants, artificers, farmers and shepherds; and each of these, again, had numerous subdivisions. Together they directed and carried out all the functions, pursuits, and industries necessary in a well-organized community.

In the sanctuary of the gods, and before the supreme power of the Pharaohs and the law, the priest, the military officer or nobleman, the merchant, the artisan, the daily laborer, the agriculturist, the shepherd, even the swineherd (considered the lowest and most unclean) —all were equal. They formed, so to say, circles rather independent than encompassed by each other. All castes had equal civil rights, and the same punishments were administered to the criminal irrespective of the caste to which he might belong. In brief, in the normal social structure of the Egyptians there existed no class deprived of the social and civil rights enjoyed by all others, or looked down upon as necessarily degraded or outlawed. The separation between one caste and another, moreover, was neither absolute nor impassable.

The ownership of the soil was unequally divided; but it was principally distributed between the sovereign, the priests, and the officer-soldiers. The latter were obliged, in consideration of the land held, to perform military services to the prince —a sort of enfeoffment like that which rose out of the chaos that succeeded the destruction of the Roman world.

Peasants, agriculturists, and yeomen, formed the bulk of the indigenous Egyptian population. The husbandmen either owned their homestead or rented the lands from the king, the priesthood, or the military caste; and they cultivated the generous soil either with their own hands or by hired field-laborers; but chattels or domestic slaves were unknown.

The primary cause of social convulsions and disturbances is always to be found in some great public calamity: such was the celebrated seven years' famine during the administration of Joseph, which resulted in concentrating in the hands of the Pharaohs numerous landed estates, and these principally the farms of the poorer yeomanry. But even then, no trace is to be discovered in history that any great proportion of the agricultural population were enslaved. Their condition then became similar, economically and socially, to that of the English peasantry during the seventeenth and eighteenth centuries; and even if it finally degenerated into something like the condition of the Fellahs, still it was simply political oppression, and not chattelhood. The modern Fellahs are serfs, enjoying all natural human rights of worship, family and property; and are separated by a wide gulf from the chattelism of modern slavery. If, like these Fellahs, the ancient Egyptians were forced to bow before the arbitrary power of a sovereign, they at least were not the personal property of an owner who had the power arbitrarily to dispose of them as his interest or caprice might dictate.

The population constituting the Egyptian nation, and included in this graded structure of castes, was of varied origin and descent, or, according to a common form of statement, belonged to various races. But the process of mixing the various ethnic elements with each other, went on uninterruptedly during the almost countless centuries of the historical existence of Egypt, including the epoch of its highest political development and the brightest blossom of its culture and civilization. In the remotest period of Egyptian society, the three superior castes were of a different hue of skin from the others, and some ethnologists and historians assign them a Shemitic or Japhetic (*i.e.*, Aryan) origin. But the optimates were not white but *red*, and so they both considered and called themselves. All the other castes-as artists, architects, merchants, mechanics, operatives, sailors, agriculturists and shepherds-undoubtedly belonged to the African or negro stock.

Egypt teemed with an active industrial population, which furnished countless soldiers to the army during long centuries of victory. Egyptian history embraces a long period of expansion. Many centuries lay between the times of the Rhameses and of Necho, during which the Egyptians conquered Nubia, Libya, and Syria, and reached Kolchis. These armies could not be recruited-and positively *were not* —from chattel slaves; for succeeding chapters will show that it was domestic slavery far more than political which tore the sinews from the arms of the nations of antiquity, and rendered defenceless their states, empires and republics. If the officers of the Egyptian armies were of a *red* extraction, the rank and file was undoubtedly of the negro family. Herodotus says that "the Egyptians were black and had short, crisped hair," and that "the skulls of the Egyptians were by far thicker than those of the Persians-so that they could scarcely be broken by a big stone, while a Persian skull could be broken by a pebble." Such were the elements, with so many, and such varied hues of skin, or pigments mixed, which constituted the Egyptian people-which formed a society so strong and compact that, for more than forty centuries, its influence and existence constitute one of the most significant phenomena of the antique world. These hybrid elements elaborated a civilization called by modern ethnologists Cushitic or Chamitic, in contradistinction to the Shemitic and to the Japhetic[4] (or Aryan.) The pre-eminent active elements in this civilization were the artists, merchants, and operatives. It was eminent for mathematical and astronomical science, for architecture, the mechanic arts, and a highly elaborated administration. And this Egyptian or Chamitic civilization, too, preceded by many centuries the Shemitic and Aryan cultures.

The origin of the denomination *Chamites* and *Cushites* has long been the subject of numerous ethnologic researches, while comparative philology, which has proved itself so potent in the solution of innumerable race-problems, has also been interrogated. The question is, by what name did the Egyptians call themselves or their land; and what meaning did they attach to such names? K-M (whence *Kam, Kem, Kemi, Cham*) signifies "the black land;" though, according to Champollion, it implies "the pure land;" while others give it the meaning of "the sceptre." At any rate, *Cham* signifies "black" in Egyptian and its ancient dialects-those of Thebes and Memphis, for instance, as also in the Coptic. Egypt proper was called by its inhabitants "the black land" on account of the appearance of its soil; it was black in contradistinction to the *red* land (or Descher, *i.e.*, "desert") which surrounded the Nile valley. The Hebrews borrowed the word from the Egyptians, and transferred it from a geographic to an ethnical name-or rather, perhaps, this application was made by subsequent commentators on the Hebrew writings. Neither was the denomination *Cush* (Egyptian *Kus, Kês-i-or, Käs*) used by the Egyptians for their own land or people. They employed it, as would appear, to denominate lands situated south of Egypt proper; for the Egyptian viceroys who administrated the government of these lands bore the title of "*Si suten n Kus,*" or king-sons of Kush. These lands were thickly inhabited by black and brown populations. In the same way, the Hebrews (or Beni-Israel) used the denominations *Cush* and *Cushites* in a generic sense for lands and tribes situated south of them; and the term expanded with the peregrinations, forced or voluntary, of the Arabs and Jews. First it was applied to lands and tribes south of Mesopotamia (Naharaina), the birthplace of Heber (Taber) and the Beni-Israel; and when they were in Egypt, either as free or captive Hycksos, they applied the term *Cush* to the region of Meroe south of the Nile; and (according to Jewish writers) Sabäa, in southern Arabia, was also inhabited by sons of Cush. It would be difficult to determine to which language the word primarily belongs, but, in all probability, early Shemitic writers transmitted it to the ancient Armenians, just as they in turn transmitted it to western or Christian writers. Herodotus used it; and his *Kissia* is identical with that of the Hebrews and Armenians. The denomination *Chute, Chuzi, Cossaia, Cussaia*, of various dialects of Fore-Asia has reference to the tribes of *Kuschani, Kusi, Cushites*. Hence Cushites are to be found in Syria, Arabia and Africa.

In the phonetic character is found the expression M-S-R as a designation for that land. It is synonymous with the Arabic *Misr*, the Jewish *Mizraim, Mazor*, and the Syriac *Mezren*. Various explanations are given of this word, according to the significations it has in the various dialects. According to some it means "stronghold," while according to others, it signifies "extension;" by the Hebrews it was applied to Egypt, or, as some commentators assert, to the Egyptians.

Other appellations for the land of Egypt are found in the hieroglyphs and in phonetic groups. This is the case, for instance, with the group *Nehi*, signifying the sycamore, which is believed to be indigenous in Egypt.

None of these names, however, had any historical signification, so that it still remains a mystery what the native name for the primitive civilizers of the Nile valley was. As for the name *Egypt, Egyptians*, this was bestowed on them by the Greeks; and some attempt to deduce it from *Phtha* or *Ptah*, a divinity of the city and township of Memphis; and the denomination, *Land of Ptah*, is supposed to have been used in a generic sense.

The advantage of thus exploring those historical and philological labyrinths will make itself clear in succeeding chapters. Philology has explained the signification of various other ancient ethnic and national names, among others, "Hebrews," "Aryas" or "Aryans," "Pelasgi," "Greeks," "Canaanites," etc., and such explanations have frequently proved of the highest value in letting us into the secret of their origin, character, and the direction of their activity. But there is no vestige of the antique language of the Egyptians that would lead us to suppose that absolute distinctions of race, or chattelhood based thereon, formed features of the primitive life in the Nile valley.

From various paintings, inscriptions, and philological data, science has endeavored to reconstruct the ethnological conceptions entertained by the Egyptians seventeen centuries B.C. The *red* race occupied Egypt (chiefly lower Egypt), Arabia, and part of Babylonia; the *yellow* race was spread over Palestine and Syria, reaching Africa; the *white* race stretched north and north-west of Egypt, inhabiting a part of Libya and the islands of Rhodes, Cyprus, Crete, etc.; the *black and brown* race occupied Egypt, Abyssinia, Nubia, and Southern Arabia. *Nah es. u* or *Nah si.*

u was the name given to all negroes or blacks who were not Egyptians, while to the whole red-colored race they applied the term *ret, ret-u*, signifying "germ."

The Egyptian pantheon was of course the creation of the superior priests. It made each human race the creation of a separate god; and very probably all the numerous elements in the complicated social structure of the Egyptians, that is, every caste or function, even the lowest, which was still an integral part of the whole, had each its separate deity. The creator of the black race was either a god represented symbolically by a blackbird, or the god H'or (or Horos), son of Osiris, and his avenger, who dwelt in the firmament with all the other deities.

The negro physiognomy appears on the Egyptian monuments; and this not only in the representations of common persons, but even in the case of kings, as, for instance, those of the eighteenth and nineteenth dynasties, in the statues of Totmes III. and Amenophis III. The Egyptian king Sabakos was an Ethiopian by birth, and many other Pharaohs married black African princesses-Nah es. u. There can be no doubt of intermarriages having been common, between *red* and *black* Egyptians proper; and through such unions, legal and illegal, it was that the brownish rather than entirely black color of the Egyptian man of the people, as represented on the monuments, was produced. (A similar slow but uninterrupted transition and modification may be verified at the present day and under our own eyes-crisped hair, thick skulls,[5] still prevailing). Finally, eunuchs are represented of a yellowish hue, perhaps nearer in tint to that of the yellow than the black race.

Some psychologic ethnologists affirm that the African or pure negro is to be considered as constituting a passive race, requiring fecundation by an active one. If this be the case, then the Egyptians solved the question. The red and dominant race drew no impassable lines of demarcation by chattelhood; and the black population formed the most vital element of the social structure.

At the threshold of what our limited knowledge considers as positive history, therefore, we meet a highly developed society and nation, which for long centuries enjoyed a political existence, normal when compared with contemporaneous and surrounding nations, and *domestic slavery neither lay at the basis of the structure, nor formed an integral element of Egyptian life.* In the monuments, paintings, and inscriptions which remain as records and reminiscences of Egypt's palmy ages, no traces are found in the regular national and domestic economy, of agricultural or industrial labor which could have been performed by slaves or chattels. Slaves and slavery existed in Egypt, not as an intrinsic and integral part of society, but as an unhealthy excrescence-not under the sanction of right or law, but as the result of a violation of both. Egyptian slavery was an atonement for social and personal crime-an abnormal monstrosity, and not the normal and vital force of Egyptian activity. If slavery had been a normal social institution, it would have had its deity and its rites; but, as exclusively the result of a disease, it was regulated and dealt with as such.

Egyptian slaves consisted of prisoners of war made on the field of battle, or captives taken in forays made into neighboring or distant countries. In early times, also, all strangers whom accident or tempest threw on the shores of Egypt, and who had no claims to a legal hospitality, were enslaved; for, for centuries Egypt was closed against the intrusion of foreigners-certain merchants and traffickers only being specially excepted. Furthermore, conquered countries paid their tribute partly in children, who thus became slaves. All these slaves were the property of the Pharaohs, who employed them in various ways, distributed them to their officials, sold them to their subjects of all castes, or to domestic and foreign traffickers. But the exportation of slaves belongs to a later period-the epoch of Egypt's historical decay. Slaves were imported, but not exported, as there was no special economical slave-breeding for this or other purposes.

It is unnecessary to dwell on the generally known fact of the captivity and enslavement of the Jews, or to detail the researches concerning the Hycksos-first slaves, then masters and rulers, and finally again overpowered and reduced to captivity. But beside these Shemites, Hebrews-be they Hycksos or not-all other races and nations were at some time or other captives and slaves in Egypt. The Pharaohs warred with Asiatics, and especially with what is now called Caucasian races; and the monuments show that red, white, and yellow slaves taken in war were far more numerous than the blacks.

Egyptians condemned for any kind of criminal offence became slaves, or were condemned to public hard labor. As equality before the law prevailed in Egypt, a person belonging to the superior caste (red-skin) was liable thus to become a slave in his own country. Contrary, however, to the custom of almost the whole of antiquity, and even of earlier Christian times, the Egyptians never reduced debtors to personal slavery. A debtor was not personally responsible, and could not be sold into slavery by his creditor.

Slaves of every kind might be redeemed and manumitted. They then became equal to other Egyptians, as is evidenced by the marriage of Joseph with a daughter of a high-priest, and by his eminent official position. Children born from Egyptians and their slave women, whether red, yellow, black or white, were equal in all rights, and shared the inheritance with the legitimate offspring of the same father. The father transmitted his own status to his children, according to a custom general in the East, and ascending to the remotest antiquity.

Slaves worked in the mines, and were employed on every kind of hard labor, but principally, and as far as possible, on those great and almost indestructible public works and monuments that distinguished the cities of the Nile. It was the pride of the Pharaohs to be enabled to inscribe on the structure that the work was not performed by the hands of Egyptians-referring to the hard work, such as carrying blocks, raising and preparing material, digging canals, etc. All the servants about the palace, sanctuary and villa were slaves. They belonged to all races and colors, and as such are represented on the monuments. In ancient, independent Egypt, therefore, slavery was, in the strictest sense, limited to the household.

Such was Egypt, the most ancient of nations and civilizations. In her, slavery was an incidental and abnormal condition, and did not enter into the vitals of society during the long centuries that this society stood foremost among nations and civilizations. In the last stages of Egyptian history, however, domestic slavery did its terrible work, helped by conquests by foreigners, by the overthrow of its independence, by exactions, tributes, and all kinds of oppressions. Then only was it that political slavery, or what is called oriental despotism, became altogether fused with domestic slavery.

Various are the causes to which the decomposition and downfall of Egypt are ascribed. Some assert that Egyptian society and civilization, traversing all the stages of growth and development, logically ended in senility, decrepitude and death. Others find in the division into castes, one of the pre-eminent causes of the decline of Egypt. But, baneful and destructive as is the organization into castes, it is a blessing when compared with domestic slavery. The rigid organization of the castes was a counter-poison, a check imposed upon the extension of domestic slavery, preventing it from eating up the healthy agencies of society. The caste system-and above all priestly caste-was, to a great extent, a curb on the despotism of the Pharaohs. The castes for many centuries prevented the fusion of the two greatest social plagues: domestic and political slavery.

The all-powerful law of analogies-which in the course of these pages will be more luminously exhibited from the fate of other empires and civilizations-authorizes already the positive, and even axiomatic assertion, that the almost unparalleled by long historical life of the Egyptians, and the highly advanced state of their civilization, are due exclusively to the fact, that domestic slavery and chattelhood remained for a long time an abnormal outgrowth. It was not the basis of domestic and national economy, not the object fit for the special care of the legislator, and was not intertwined with the social, political and intellectual life of the Egyptians.

18

II. Phœnicians

AUTHORITIES:

Moevers, Rénan, Duncker, Ewald, Ezekiel, Proverbs of Solomon, etc.

Previous to any epoch settled by positive history, the Canaanites, or Phœnicians, a highly civilized nation, dwelt in the land called Palestine. They were an elderly branch of the Shemitic family; their generic name embracing the Hittites, Jebusites, Amorites, and Girgasites-all of whom the Greeks called *Phœnicians*. *Canaan*, in the Shemitic dialects, signifies "lowland," as was Palestine, in contradistinction to *Aram*, or the highlands of Mesopotamia (*Naharajim*, *Nahirim* of the Old Testament). *Canaan*, in Hebrew proper, is sometimes synonymous with "merchant;" and the historical development of the Phœnicians explains and justifies this signification. The Greek name *Phœnicians*, is supposed by some to be derived from *phoinizai*, "to kill," whence *Phoinikes* (Phœnicians), "bloody men." The Phœnicians, being very jealous of their maritime trade, killed and in every way molested the navigators from other lands who dared to follow their vessels or spy out their extensive maritime establishments, factories, or connections. For this reason the Greeks long considered the Tyrrenian seas as highly dangerous for navigators, and as filled with rocks, monsters, and anthropophagi. Other investigators, again, derive the Greek word Phœnicians from their *ruddy* complexion, or from their having first navigated the Red Sea.

The primitive seats of the Phœnicians lay north and south of Syria. From thence they are supposed to have emigrated to Palestine through the northern part of Syria, while another column from the south advanced from the delta on the Persian Gulf, anciently called *Assyrium Stagnum*, or from the islands of Tyros (Tylos) and Arados, situated in the above-named waters. Some writers suppose that an earthquake obliged them to emigrate from these shores of the Erythrean or Red Sea (Persian Gulf) of antiquity, and that their Greek name owes its origin to this circumstance.

These wanderings through regions already thickly inhabited by various tribes and nations, may have contributed to develop in these Shemites that powerful mercantile propensity to which they chiefly owe their historical immortality; then and there, too, they most probably began the traffic in slaves, to which, if they were not its originators, they certainly gave a new and powerful impulse. Thus, while the Phœnicians figure in history as the earliest navigators and merchants, they must also be written down in the light of having inaugurated, or at least, greatly extended the accursed slave-trade.

No division into castes seems ever to have existed among the Phœnicians. As a general rule, no traces of this social circumscription are to be detected among the nations of pure or even of mixed Shemitic stock which flourished in Fore-Asia —in Syria, Babylon or Assyria. The Phœnician political organism embraced 1st, the powerful ruling families; and 2dly, the subject classes —a division similar to that of the *aristos* and *demos* which prevailed in Greece, or to the patricians and plebeians of Rome. The land of Canaan was originally cultivated by freeholders and yeomen. When one tribe subdued another, or when the victors settled among the vanquished, the latter were not enslaved; they became a kind of tribute-paying colonists, with limited political privileges, but with full civil rights. They were at liberty to hold real and personal property of every kind, just as much as the ruling tribe or class. So also it was among all the Shemites, and, with but few exceptions, among all the nations of antiquity.

Slaves, at this period, were employed only at hard labor in the cities and in the household; they were as yet neither farmers, field-laborers, nor mechanics. But, as already mentioned, the Phœnicians were the great slave-traders, carriers and factors in the remotest antiquity, and this both by land and sea. At a period of more than fourteen centuries B.C., the Phœnicians covered all the shores around the Egean and Mediterranean seas with their factories, strongholds and colonial cities. Besides this, they stretched out even to the Euxine, while their colonies studded, also, the Corinthian and Ionian gulfs (on the sites of modern Patras and Lepanto), and extended on the Atlantic coast even beyond Gibraltar. The records of the earliest wanderings of these Canaanitish tribes into Africa, and even Greece, are preserved in legends as the migrations of gods, demigods and heroes.

Thus the Phœnicians linked in a vast commercial chain Britain, Iberia (Spain), and India; while the Guadalquiver, the Nile, the Euphrates, the Tigris and the Indus, served as highways for their trading enterprise. From Byblos, Tyre, Sidon and other emporiums, they sent out caravans far and wide into Arabia and Fore-Asia. The products of their art and industry were reputed most exquisite even as early as the epoch of the Iliad, and they were vain enough to look on themselves as the pivots of the world's prosperity, and the Scriptures repeatedly mention the pride and denounce the vices of the Phœnician cities. What their merchants bought or received in barter in Asia or in Egypt, they exchanged for the rough products of Greece, Spain, Albion, Libya, and the lands on the Euxine: these consisted principally of grains, hides, copper, tin, silver, gold, and indeed all kinds of marketable objects. Their central situation for the commerce of the known and almost of the unknown world, especially favored the slave-trade. Accordingly Phœnician slaves became more and more valuable, and a continually extending market produced a constantly increasing demand. In all probability the inland caravan excursions afforded the principal supplies for their immense slave traffic; but they also bought, stole, and kidnapped from every possible place and by every conceivable stratagem-just as modern American slave-traders do. In this horrid industry they visited every shore. They carried it on among the Greeks, among the Barbarians of the Hellespont and the Pontus, among the Iberians, Italians, Moors and other Africans. Natives of Asia were sold to Greece and other European countries, while Syria and Egypt were furnished with European slaves. The great majority of these slaves belonged to what is called the Caucasian race, and negroes constituted a comparatively insignificant part. In return for these white chattels the Phœnicians bartered the products of Egypt and of Fore-Asia.

The Phœnicians, then, were the great, and, in all probability, the exclusive slave-traders of those times. The traffic had its chief centre in Byblos, Sidon and Tyre-the depots, bazaars, and storehouses of which were always glutted with human merchandise.

In times positively historical, when Phœnicia had come to be the mighty and flourishing emporium of the world's trade, foreign slaves constituted the immense majority of the population of her cities-as indeed was the case with most of the commercial cities of antiquity; but none of them were so crowded with slaves as were Byblos, Tyre, and Sidon. In consequence of this agglomeration, slavery gradually crept from the market and the household into general industry and agriculture. The slaves thus employed by the Phœnicians may be classified as follows: 1. Slaves of luxury, living in the house of the master; 2. Slaves employed in various branches of manufacture, as weavers, dyers, and artisans of all kinds-as also in the manual labors common to every maritime and commercial city; 3. Agricultural slaves.

This vast accumulation of slaves begat repeated and bloody revolts during the whole historic existence of Phœnicia. The scanty and comparatively insignificant fragments of her history which now exist are filled with accounts of such revolts, generally ending as most fearful tragedies. An uprising of this kind occurred in Tyre about ten centuries B.C.; and history records, that at that time the king, the aristocracy, all the masters, and even great numbers of non-slaveholding freemen were slaughtered. The women, however, were saved and married by the slaves; and thus many primitive oligarchic families entirely disappeared. Frequent servile revolts and insurrections of this kind resulted at length in the partial emancipation of the slaves and their conquest of certain civil rights.

In keeping with the almost boundless accumulation of wealth in those cities was the increase in the number of slaves. As a consequence, the free laborers, artisans, and farmers became impoverished and dispossessed; and, as was natural, they often joined the insurgent bondmen. The oligarchs also sent out these poor freemen wherever Phœnician ships could carry them, or wherever there was a chance of establishing factories, cities, or colonies. Such was the common origin of those primitive Phœnician settlements, which were scattered north and west on almost every shore. In most regions, even in Libya, their object was simply commercial and not at all of a conquering character. At any rate the newcomers soon intermarried and mixed with the natives.

The slaveholding rulers were now forced to sustain a hired soldiery to keep down the slaves-not for defence against an external but an internal foe. Among these hirelings were the Carryians, Lydians, Libyans, and Libyo-Phœnicians. To such motley mercenaries were they obliged to intrust the security of their homes and municipalities. At times this hireling soldiery joined the revolted slaves, and they formed but a poor defence against the Egyptians, or against Assyrian, Babylonian, Persian, and Alexandrian conquest. To all these empires the Phœnician slaveholders were obliged to pay tribute, until finally Alexander massacred or enslaved them all-slaveholders and slaves alike.

Already some of the violent pro-slavery militants in the slave section of the United States express their purpose to invoke the aid of France in their schemes of secession and conquest, and propose that their cities and states be occupied by French garrisons. What a striking analogy with the course of the fated Phœnicians! And if eventually France should listen to their humble prayer and send defenders to these terrified slave-masters, climatic reasons would induce her to furnish such troops as are naturally fitted to bear the tropical heats of the slave-coast —the malarious regions of Louisiana and South Carolina. Such would be her Zouaves and Turcos-the Zouaves enemies of every kind of slavery, and the Turcos negroes themselves. Where then would be their defenders and their security? Every French soldier, even if neither Zouave nor Turco, would, in all probability, side at once with the oppressed against the oppressor. The prejudice of race, so prevalent in America, is not a European characteristic: it did not exist in antiquity; it does not prevail in Europe now.

It was not the existence of an oriental political despotism in Phœnicia-it was *domestic slavery*, which, penetrating into industry and agriculture, destroyed the richest, most enterprising, and most daring community of remote antiquity. Cicero wrote their epitaph: *"Fallacissimum esse genus Phœnicum, omnia monumenta vetustatis atque omnes historia nobis prodiderunt."*

When, therefore, positive history slowly rises on the limitless horizon of time, Phœnicia appears as an ominous illustration of how domestic slavery, from an external social monstrosity, tends to become a chronic but corrosive disease. And neither does the evidence of history end with her. Over and over again will it be found that slavery, after eating so deeply into the social organism as to become constitutional and chronic, has the same ultimate issue, even as a virus slowly but surely penetrates from the extremities into the vitals of the animal organism.

The intermediate stages of such diseases and the process of the symptoms are often modified in their outward manifestations to such an extent as to lead even the keen observer astray. But it is only he who can unerringly diagnosticate the *nature* of the disease who can ever become a great healer: he discovers the true character and source of the malady, whatever may be its external complications, and from whatever conditions and influences they may result. Some symptoms may increase, others decrease in intensity and virulence in the physiological as in the social dis-ease-they are, however, secondary. The parallel holds good-the principle remaining unchanged: life becomes extinct for similar reasons in the animal as in the social and political body.

Thus, in the history of the Phœnicians, and therefore, in the earliest authentic epoch, a great historical and social law manifests itself in full action. This activity it retains through all the subsequent social and political catastrophes in the life of nations and empires, down even to Hayti with her immortal Toussaint. *Slavery generates bloody struggles.* Many of these have resulted in the slaves violently regaining their liberty, while others have destroyed the whole state-swallowing up the slaveholders in their own blood, or burying them under the ruins of their own social edifice.

III. Libyans

AUTHORITIES:

Diodorus Siculus, Corippus, Moevers, etc.

The primitive social and intellectual condition of the populations dwelling along the shores of Africa washed by the Mediterranean sea, can only be inferred from their respective relations with the Phœnicians and Carthaginians. Other sources of historical information as to that remote period there are none, while later times also give comparatively scanty satisfaction.

Ethnology has not yet positively determined who the aborigines of Libya were, and it is questionable if it can ever be satisfactorily settled. Egyptian inscriptions indicate a white race in the north-eastern corner of Libya, adjoining Egypt; while further to the west lived the blacks. At a period exceedingly remote, the whites mixed with these negro blacks, who probably immigrated from the centre of Africa-Soudan-and spread over the whole of Libya. These remote epochs, however, altogether refuse chronological limitation. But when chronology, even of the most rudimentary kind, becomes possible, history shows us the existence, in Libya, of a nomadic and agricultural people, who can be no other than these cross-breeds, and who had brought a part of the land to a high degree of cultivation. The Libyans may thus be considered as an autochthonous African population—a theory which is confirmed by other evidence not now necessary to give.

Among these Libyans-called by the Greeks *Afri*, and by the Romans, *Africani*—agriculture was in a highly flourishing condition at the epoch of the earliest myths and legends of Greece: all the Hellenic legends relating to the distant sea-wanderings of gods or heroes, carry them to the Libyan shores about the *Regio Syrtica*—Tripolis. Among these are the Argonauts and Heraklides, Perseus, Kadmos, Odysseus, and Menalaos. So the Greek myths of Atlas and the Garden of the Hesperides have their spring and source in that part of Libya. All this presupposes a very old culture. Herodotus says that the Ægis of the Greek Pallas originated in Libya, as also that Athene here received Gorgona's head for her Ægis. Even at the present day, the chiefs of some of the tribes in the southern part of ancient Libya carry the skins of leopards and other wild beasts on their shoulders in such a way that the head of the animal, Ægis-like, covers their breast. The adventurous Phœnician and Greek navigators of the earliest period accordingly found the Libyans already a highly cultivated people. This culture, too, they possessed previous to their intercourse with the Canaanites, Phœnicians, or Greeks-anterior even to the wanderings of Astarte, Anna, or Dido.

At this epoch the Libyans were possessed of written language. Their alphabet was, in certain peculiarities, of an older type than even the Phœnician-that father of so many eastern and western alphabets. *Leptis* and *Oka* are Libyan names for Libyan cities which were in existence previous to any Phœnician colonizations-though these colonizations are themselves anterior to positive history.

Goats, sheep, and other domestic animals were introduced into Greece and Italy from Libya; and from thence also came the knowledge of how to breed and rear them. The Libyans also, in all probability, first taught them the mode of keeping and rearing bees, as the Greek word for "wax," *keros*—Latin, *cera*, is by some deduced from the Berber (Libyan) *ta-kir*, and the Greek designation for honey, *meli, mel*—Latin, *mel*, from the Berber *ta-men-t*. Others, however, trace both those words to a Sanscrit root.

As an evidence of their advanced civilization, it may be mentioned that the Libyans were highly accomplished in horticulture at a time when the fields of Greece and Italy were only rudely ploughed. From Libya across the Mediterranean, the leguminous or pulse plants seem to have been introduced into Southern Europe, together with the mode of their use and culture; and some investigators consider that the Latin names for "pease" (*cicer*), for "lentils" (*lens, lentis*), and for "beans" (*faba*), have their origin in the Berber *ikiker, ta-linit*, and *fabua*. But to these words, also, others give a Sanscrit origin. *Cucurbis* "cucumber," is in Berber *curumb*—although, again, it is traced, but forcedly, to the Sanscrit. Whatever may be the origin of the words, it is an historical fact that the Romans acquired their whole knowledge of horticulture from the Libyans and Libyo-Phœnicians; and it may even be surmised that the Latin *urtus*, "hortus," had its root in the Berber *urt*.

Civilization among the Libyans, therefore, was anterior to any contact either with Phœnicians or Greeks, and long centuries anterior to the Carthaginian domination over the northern shores of Africa.

The Libyans were a nation of agriculturists and freeholders. No trace of slavery appears among them, and, if it existed at all, was altogether insignificant and accidental. When the Phœnicians and Canaanitish settlements increased in power and number, the Libyans became tributary colonists, and the Phœnicians instituted the slave-trade among them, whose victims were confined mostly to the nomads.

As we have before said, the poor white colonists sent from Canaan and Phœnicia to Libya intermarried with the natives; and from this union came the Libyo-Phœnicians of history. The relations which the Libyans (and subsequently the Libyo-Phœnicians, when again subjugated) held to Phœnician and Canaanitish settlers, were similar to those which free Romans afterward held to the Longobard and Frankish conquerors who settled upon and held the lands of which they were once the masters.

IV. Carthaginians

AUTHORITIES:

Dionysius of Halicarnassus, Polybius, Corippus, Moevers, etc.

The Carthaginians were the great ethnic offshoots of Phœnicia in the western part of the ancient world. It would not be in place here to inquire what motives led these wanderers away from their Asiatic home, or what was the nature of the settlement which they made. They left Tyre and founded the celebrated city of Carthage, on a spot where an ancient colony from Sidon previously existed.[6] Carthage very early-indeed, we might almost say, at the start-assumed a higher character than any previous colony or city of Phœnicia. It soon became, in fact, an independent political power. It began to flourish at a time when Tyre and Sidon were on the decline, and when these once great cities had become tributary to Asiatic potentates. The Carthaginians became first the protectors, and soon afterward, the masters of all the ancient Phœnician colonies scattered over the western world. Nor did they stop here; they became a warlike and conquering empire. The political misfortunes of their mother country increased, by almost uninterrupted immigration, the number of poor free citizens in Carthage, as well as in other seacoast cities now Punic, though once Phœnician-many of them, indeed, having a numerous Libyo-Phœnician population. This surplus the Carthaginians sent off as colonists into the interior of Libya, where they founded smaller cities or settled as agriculturists among the native population, whose lands, in many instances, were assigned to the new-comers. The Carthaginian oligarchy soon began to oppress and look with contempt upon the ancient Phœnicians, Libyo-Phœnicians and Libyans. In process of time, the new colonists mixed with the ancient populations, and all were soon equally sufferers from oppressive tributes and exactions. The common hatred of these various populations against the oligarchy, which frequently led to revolt, was a powerful aid to the Numidian kings and to the Romans in their efforts to crush haughty Carthage.

The great Carthaginian oligarchs and slaveholders extended and perfected what the Phœnicians perhaps only began. They acquired in various ways vast landed estates, and oppressed and impoverished the tributary colonists and small freeholders by grievous exactions; they seized their homesteads, and finally reduced them to serfdom and slavery. Toward the decline of Carthaginian power, such estates were mostly cultivated by slaves; and these slaves-those in the country as well as those in the cities-were either Libyo-Phœnicians and Libyans, or belonged to Asiatic and European races-the unhappy individuals being either bought or taken as prisoners of war. The subdued and slave populations were as mixed as the Carthaginian armies, which, in Africa especially, contained a vast number of negroes-thus presenting an antetype of the French Turcos.

The gigantic struggle of Carthage with Rome decided the destinies of the world. Carthage fell. But the breath of the moribund slave-holding oligarchy of Carthage poisoned Rome. The tragic malediction of Dido received its fulfilment, though not in the precise manner recorded by Virgil in the Ænead.

After having conquered Carthage and Numidia, the Romans distributed among their own colonists the immense estates of the Carthaginian slaveholders, which, however, had been previously appropriated by the Numidian kings. Phœnicians, Libyo-Phœnicians, Libyans and Carthaginians, all now either became Roman colonists, or else serfs and chattels in the villas of their Roman masters. When the Vandals conquered Africa, the Romans in their turn shared the fate of all their predecessors, who had in succession been reduced to serfdom and domestic slavery, the one by the other. In the character of serfs and chattels, these various races now cultivated for their Vandal masters the lands and farms which once were their own. Thus affording an additional illustration of the eternal and omnipotent law of *retribution* and *compensation*.

V. Hebrews, or Beni-Israel

AUTHORITIES:

The Scriptures, Ewald, Rénan, Duncker, Gessenius, Grotefend, etc.

The pro-slavery party, pacific as well as militant, has long sought to fall back on the Mosaic records for the justification of the "sacred" and "patriarchal" institution. The historic records throw a bright light on the gray dawn of Hebraic life-giving us an insight into the primitive forms of society, not only of the Hebrews, but of the other, and especially the Shemitic inhabitants of Syria and of Fore-Asia. And, truly enough, servants and slaves are found around the tent of the patriarch.

It has already been mentioned that in times long prior to any definite chronology, the regions constituting Syria, Palestine and Arabia were inhabited by various tribes-some of whom were offshoots from one stem and some from another. Of these tribes, some had already formed themselves into well-developed societies, while others, if they were not absolutely roving nomads, yet often changed their dwellings according to the exigencies of pastoral life. Palestine, the final home of the Hebrew, was, in all probability, the earliest as well as the chief highway of antiquity-especially for the Shemitic and Chamitic races, just as the Caucasus and its slopes are supposed to have been the highway for Aryan or Indo-European emigrants, and for Finnic, Altaïc, and Mongolian or yellow races. This character it had before the time when Terah, Abraham's father, drove his herds from the table-lands of Mesopotamia (*Naharaina*); and it preserved it under Phœnician as well as under Hebrew dominion. Repeatedly did Egyptians, Assyrians and Babylonians, as well as Persians, and finally Alexander and his generals, march through Palestine in their invading and conquering expeditions. The important part which Palestine played in the early commercial history of the world, also, has already been pointed out while treating of the Phœnicians.

The origin first of domestic servitude, and then of absolute chattelhood, among the primitive pastoral tribes, may be traced to two distinct sources, both of them springing from abnormal conditions and events. One source was the constant feuds and wars of the tribes; the other, individual indolence and shiftlessness. The household of a patriarch, originally composed of a family and then of a clan, soon had its share of restless as well as indolent dependents. Such hangers-on were neither as frugal nor as industrious as the patriarch's family, and so enjoyed but small consideration; generally, moreover, they were most likely strangers who, through necessity or gratitude, adhered to the house and considered themselves an integral part of it. But the patriarch had the most absolute power over all the members of the family-over his wife, his sons and daughters, and all their progeny and relations. He could banish them from the family and hearth; he could sell them away to others; he had power of life and death over them all; and such powers, of course, extended over dependents and servants. In fact, the patriarch was the supreme and only-existing law. His will, and absolute obedience thereto, was the only guarantee of order inside of the tent, and outside of it also in their relations with the tents and clans of other patriarchs. The more exclusive and distinct such a family or clan was, the more independent it was in all its relations with similar social crystallizations; and the more closely did the dependents adhere to it for support and protection.

Such was undoubtedly the origin of the domestic servitude which appears in the Scriptures with the apparition of Abraham as a distinct historical individuality. But such servants and dependents being a part of the family, were not commonly sold nor made an article of merchandise, and were not, strictly speaking, chattels, as were prisoners made in feuds or wars.[7] Besides, in the formation of the primitive patriarchal household, the domestic, pastoral and agricultural labors were performed by the family-children, grandchildren, etc.; just as it is in the present day in every simple household-for a simple family formed the germ of the tribe and of the retainers around the tent of the patriarch. As the family increased, so did the herds, and so also did the duties to be performed. Meanwhile the members of the expanding family continued to attend to the household services-just as is now the case in similar circumstances-without their becoming slaves or chattels for all that. The primitive Aryan language (of which hereafter) clearly confirms what both reason and analogy assert as being an inherent fact in the constitution of every family, whatever may be the peculiarities of skin or skull, or their other ethnic characteristics. Moreover, even according to those opposed to the absolute unity of the whole human race, the Shemites descend from the same common progenitor as the Aryas (of whom are we), and this affinity strengthens what was said above concerning the similarity of their domestic life.

With the increase of the tribes and families, neighboring or scattered, increased the degeneracy of the dependents, until finally these miserable persons, grown to be an excrescence on the primitive Hebrew family life, and unable to take care of themselves, willingly accepted slavery-at times indeed craved it. The same phenomenon, under different modifications, and occasioned by various causes, again and again reappears in divers nations and empires, just as the same bodily maladies have constantly reproduced themselves throughout the countless centuries of human existence. And indeed the *morale* of Noah's curse can only be, that servitude, being generated by corruption of manhood, was, in its very nature, a diseased and degraded condition.

Abraham belonged to a class common to the Arabs, Hebrews, and all the Shemitic races-shieks or chiefs of warlike tribes, who were in the habit of making war against each other, carrying off prisoners, and even kidnapping on occasion. It was these victims chiefly that were the objects of traffic; and this very trait is true of the Arab tribes down to the present day.

The Hebrews, liberated from captivity in Egypt-that is, from political slavery, which must never be confounded with chattelhood-fought against their kinsmen, the Shemitic Canaanites, with a view to make themselves a home in a country already thickly settled, and in comparatively advanced culture and civilization. The Hebrews, poor, energetic, and hardened by the privations of a long captivity, bore the same relation to the nations of Canaan which they invaded, as the half-naked, half-starved barbarians of a long subsequent epoch bore to the Roman world, against which they rushed with the force of doom. The invading Israelites, according to the commands of Jahveh (Jehovah), carried on wars of extermination against the Phœnicians, Philistines, Ammonites, Amorites, Moabites, and other inhabitants of south-western Syria. Many of these original occupants and cultivators of the land of Canaan fled even to Africa, from the exterminating fury of the Jews, led by Moses, Aaron, and Joshua. Meanwhile the Jews took possession of the conquered and abandoned lands, which were divided between the tribes; and the great body of the Hebrews settled on them as agriculturists and free yeomen. In process of time, under the direction and inspiration of Jahveh, the supreme Lord of Israel, the body of commandments, regulations and ceremonials, called the Mosaic law, was framed.

The law of Moses has two prominent divisions-first, imperative commands, and second, dispensations. In respect of all absolute duties to God, as well as domestic and social duties, the law lays down its commands even to the minutest details, and rigidly condemns their violator. But, on the other hand, taking into account human frailty, and the temptations to which it is exposed, as also the exigencies and customs of life, the law is also full of dispensations. This twofold character of the Mosaic law affords its antagonists a broad field for assaults on its apparent contradictions. The law condemns idolatry, yet Aaron, the first high-priest, casts a golden calf for the people to worship, while Moses raises a brazen serpent before their eyes as a material symbol for their faith. The law commands monogamy, but permits and regulates concubinage. It prohibits licentiousness, fornication, and rape, but overlooks them in certain instances, as, for example, after a successful battle or the storming of a city, because such crimes are unavoidable when the demoniac passions are brought powerfully into play. Many other illustrations of this twofold character of the Mosaic law might be pointed out.

But minute and precise though the Mosaic record is in its religious and social commands and obligations, it nowhere commands the Hebrews, as a religious or social duty, to enslave the Canaanitish idolaters among whom they lived. Enslavement and chattelhood are nowhere laid down as special duties, nor is slavery regarded as forming the corner-stone of the Jewish social, civil, and religious structure. Slavery is not the subject of the covenant with God or of the covenant with man; neither did the possession of slaves confer any political, religious, or social rights. All this was left for the deduction of modern theology and politics.

The Mosaic law deals with slavery as with an existing evil, and regulates it as an abnormal institution. The lawgiver recalls to the memory of the Jews that they were themselves captives and bondsmen-an historic fact to which, as we have already seen, the ancestry of many of the slaveholders in the United States, at the present day, furnish a parallel.

But perhaps Biblical commentators have not drawn with sufficient severity the distinction in meaning between the Hebrew word for "servant," "attendant," etc., and that for an "absolute chattel." Chattelhood, in the modern legal and practical application of the term, was undoubtedly a rare condition in the time of the patriarchs, and even in the primitive theocratic epochs of Beni-Israel. The Hebrew language has four words to express the primitive domestic relations of the race, and neither of them will admit the meaning of positive chattelhood. Probably the oldest is the word *a'buddah*, which occurs in the book of Job, whose dialect is considered by modern philologists to be far older than the Mosaic scriptures; the same word is also found once only in Genesis (Gessenius Dict.). It is a collective noun, and signifies "attendants," "laborers," and, according to some exegetes, it also signifies an *"estate."* Such may perhaps be its meaning in the book of Job, as it occurs after the enumeration of various movables, such as flocks and herds, and may thus, in distinction, convey the idea of real property. The logical sequence in such enumerations was undoubtedly the same then as it is now-movables first in order, then landed property. Another Hebrew word for the primitive domestic servant is *na'ar*, but its application seems to have been rather limited; it is mostly employed to designate a "lad-servant" or "apprentice." The word most generally used, however, and the one most variously translated and explained by lexicographers is *e'bed*: it variously signifies "subject," "servant," "serf," "slave," "attendant," "officer," etc. Its application to a "serf" or "slave" has perhaps rather a moral or ideal than a positive legal or social sense. Thus, when in Genesis it is said that "Moses removed the swarms of flies from Pharaoh, from his servants (*e'bed*), and from his people," the word *e'bed* undoubtedly signifies "ministers," "courtiers," "officers," and "servants of the court," and not actual serfs or slaves. Common sense would surely indicate that chattels could not have been mentioned immediately after the great Pharaoh, and before his people; and still less likely is it that the oriental despotism which reduced *all* to political slaves was unknown in the Egypt of the early Pharaohs. Finally, the word *abduh* alone may signify a "slave" in the strict sense of the term; it is used by Ezra, and belongs to a period of national degradation, when both slavery and idolatry flourished in Israel.

Slavery, however, never became an integral element of Hebrew life, nor, during their centuries of glory, did its pestilence-breath endanger the national vitality. The Mosaic record, covering a period of nearly one thousand years, never mentions any slave revolt, such as so often shook the neighboring and contemporaneous Phœnicians.

For domestic slaves, the Hebrews procured foreigners, through traffic or by war; and such slaves were of the same race as the slaves of the Phœnicians and other neighboring nations. In the history of the Beni-Israel, there are long episodes containing accounts of wars, principally with tribes belonging to the same Shemitic family from which the Hebrews themselves sprang, and many of the slaves made in these wars must have belonged to the nearest cities and kingdoms. If these had been so numerous as to be employed in large bodies in agricultural labor, undoubtedly there would have been revolts during the absence of their masters on military expeditions, or even during times of peace. The absence of any such event in the history of the Hebrews, proves that domestic slavery was for many long centuries recognized only as an abnormal institution, and its growth circumscribed by jubilees and limitary statutes.

The regulations prescribing the status of slaves, and their general condition, are within, the reach of every one. Their spirit is mild and beneficent for the bond-man; the duration of his slavery is limited-his treatment is humane, and the condition not ordinarily hereditary. In the times of the early patriarchs, a servant could become the chief of the family-thus proving that some commentators have made a strange confusion in the interpretation of the above-mentioned Hebrew word (*e'bed*), when they construe it as applying to such a system as modern American slavery. A servant who was eligible to become the chief of a family could not be a chattel, but must necessarily have been a member of the clan, with independent powers and rights, and at least the proprietorship of himself.

Among the Hebrews, also, a man could voluntarily sell himself into slavery; thus the debtor paid his debts with his own body, or with that of his wife or child. This custom was almost universal in early antiquity, as well as among the Romans and the barbarous Germans. But the Mosaic law appointed a regular epoch for the emancipation of all slaves, and therefore of debtors among the rest; and the operation of this law it was which made hereditary slavery of such comparatively rare occurrence.

Slaves, therefore, even when bought from the Gentiles, and therefore considered *unclean* by the Hebrews, or when prisoners taken in war, were not cut off from the general law of protection. They enjoyed human rights, and some of the civil privileges of the Jewish born. No absolute distinctions of men can be traced in the Mosaic law without perverting its whole moral tendency. When a slave received any severe wound from his master, he was from thence declared free, and the Jewish law punishes with death the sale of a freeman into slavery —(a fact, by the way, in striking contrast with the great social movement of the militant pro-slavery party, whose policy it is to enslave both emancipated and free-born). A slave concubine could not be sold to strangers-still less her children by her master. But if he wished to be rid of her, the master was obliged to find her a husband or another master among his relatives or friends. In the old colonial times in America, the law inflicted a penalty on *white servants and bondsmen* for mixing with black chattels-but what penalty threatened the *white masters* for the same offence? The fact is, the slave-breeders of the slave regions continually invoke the Bible to justify their doings, and continually violate Scriptural regulations.

The Mosaic law commands: "Thou shalt not deliver unto his master the servant which is escaped from his master unto thee: he shall dwell with thee, even among you, in the place which he shall choose in one of thy gates, where it liketh him best: thou shalt not oppress him." Some modern commentators attempt to contract this humane and universal command, by arguing that it only applied to *Jewish born* servants or slaves; but sound criticism utterly annihilates the assumption. On the contrary, the phrase "*in one of thy gates*," is a positive proof that the command had in view fugitives of every tribe and kingdom. All Gentiles, slaves as well as freemen, were considered by the Jews "unclean," and there might have been some difficulty in admitting such runaways into their *houses*. But whatever was the creed or nationality of the *escaped*, he found safety "*in the gates*," and from thence could not be "delivered unto his master." Difference of religion and not of race constituted the paramount distinction between the Jew and the Gentile; if the command, therefore, were exclusively applicable to the Jewish slave, even then its spirit is violated by the American fugitive slave act, to uphold which, the Mosaic law is blasphemed-for the enslaved race of Christian America are of the same faith and baptism as their owners.

With the increase of luxury and corruption under the Hebrew kings, kidnapping and the traffic in men and women seem to have largely increased. The slaves stolen in piratical expeditions among neighboring tribes were exported to a distance, while others were imported from thence into Judea. But against this practice the prophets-those inspired successors of the lawgiver of Sinai-thundered terribly. The Edomites and other Phœnicians-who seem to have been pre-eminently the slave-traders of their time-importing slaves from Gaza, which was then a great thoroughfare and commercial metropolis, and exporting them to other points, were declared to be the most accursed of nations. So now, the modern Edomites of this continent, who have again revived the slave-traffic between Africa and this country, together with all who aid, abet, patronize or excuse them, come under the curse so often denounced against their ancient prototypes.

Under the kings, also, domestic slavery became more extensive, and its influence more fatal. It did not yet, however, succeed in devouring the vitals of the nation, or wholly destroying the small homesteads and the free yeomanry, as it afterward did in Greece, and over almost the entire ancient world under republican and imperial Rome. The epoch of the kings is one of moral degradation and effeminacy on the one hand, and of disasters and captivities to the Jews themselves, on the other. Sensuality and general depravity flourished rank and wild under the malignant influence of domestic slavery. Slavery relaxed the ties of family and society among the Jews, as history shows it to have done in every place and in all ages of its existence-for slavery, sensuality and general depravity mutually engender and sustain each other. But in their deepest and most helpless degradation, the Jews never sold the offspring of their own personal lechery into slavery: this advance on the turpitude of Hebraic slavery-this outrage on the humanity of the faith we inherit from the Jews-was first justified and systematized by the slave states of the great Republic of the West! In ancient as in Christian times, there were doubtless parents who abandoned their legitimate or illegitimate offspring to public mercy, to accident, or to servitude; but all legislators have condemned such inhumanity, and tried, if possible, to regulate and soften it. So, deliberate selling of one's children may anciently have occurred in solitary instances; but it was always and everywhere condemned as the sum of all infamies.

Many of the tutelary regulations for the slaves laid down in the law, fell, it is true, into disuse, even as other parts of the law were violated by the wayward and stiff-necked Israelites. On the advent to power of the good Josiah, however, the violated commandments and regulations of Moses, including those concerning the slaves, were rigidly enforced, and a general reformation inaugurated.

The increase of wealth, the various modifications and changes generated in the organism of society by its growth, as also by wars, captivities, changes of government, etc., brought forth a new subordinate condition in the domestic and civil life of the Hebrews-it was that of the *client*, and belongs to the latter epoch of the kings. Theologians of doubtful learning, and still more dubious honesty, argue that such clients were slaves; but, in truth, the clients among the Hebrews were no more the slaves of their patrons than the same class were among the Romans or Gauls. The Hebrew client was a *subordinate*, but *independent*; he was under the protection of his patron, but both were bound by mutual obligations and prescribed conditions; and the property and estate of the patron were often under the guardianship of the client. Many expressions in the Scriptures, also, bearing on the mission of the future Messianic servant of Jahveh, mean properly a client, and not a slave or a chattel.

The old kingdom of Judea was overthrown in wars with Assyria and Babylon; and the Jews were carried away as captives. These repeated captivities chiefly befell the most wealthy and influential part of the population. Such captives generally became political slaves, that is, were deprived of political, though not of religious or civil rights, and were not made domestic slaves or chattels. They became the property of the king or of the state; but were not individually subject to be scattered or sold; in fact, they became colonists, and lands were assigned them in some part of the empire. Thus Tiglath-Palassar colonized certain regions north of Nineveh with Hebrews; and Sargon (or Sargina) transplanted others to Media. In the Babylonian captivities their condition was precisely similar: thus, when Cyrus liberated forty-two thousand three hundred and sixty Jews from captivity in Babylon, there were among them only seven thousand three hundred and eighty-seven slaves, or about one-sixth of the whole number.

Domestic slavery, as we have seen, made considerable havoc among the Beni-Israel, and its life was continually recruited by wars and the consequent ruin and impoverishment of the people, as well as by other causes already pointed out. But down to the last breath of the political and national existence of the Jews-to the day of the destruction of Jerusalem and the hour of final dispersion-slavery never succeeded in wholly destroying the humble homesteads of the free rural population-as it did in other nations and empires of antiquity: for example, it never extirpated the free agricultural yeomanry in Palestine as it afterward did in the Roman world, from the Atlantic to the Euphrates. The free population was mostly devoted to agriculture, and possessed homesteads; and these small free homesteads were regarded almost as sacred–even kings could only by violence seize upon the poor man's farm.

Little Palestine, to the East, swarmed like a beehive with people, notwithstanding captivities, calamities, and exterminating wars. At the time of David, the kingdom of Palestine was about the size of the present kingdom of Portugal, and had a population of about three million eight hundred thousand. Under Solomon, his son, fifty-three thousand six hundred foreign-born slaves worked at the construction of the temple, most of whom, probably, were the property of the king or of the state–not private chattels. If we allow that the number of Jewish-born slaves of both sexes and of all ages was even four times as large (which is not at all likely, considering the source and means of supply of slaves), it will give only two hundred and sixty-eight thousand slaves of every type, in Judea, or one-fourteenth part of the population.[8]

How corrupt soever the law and its regulations became, both, nevertheless, remained a check upon domestic slavery. Long previous to the terrible Flavian epoch, the Hebrews were thickly scattered over the eastern and western world, not as exported slaves, but as wanderers and adventurers: there may, indeed, have been slaves among them, but such slaves formed the minority. Strangers, indeed, they were, but free according to then existing municipal limitations. It was the surplus of a free population that thus wandered abroad in search of better fortunes —a phenomenon which is reproduced in the present day by the immigration to America of the surplus population of various European states. So large was this emigration that, in the time of Cicero, the Jews, Italians and Greeks formed the principal nationalities that took part in the tumults of the Roman forum, and on one occasion they hooted Cicero while on the rostrum. The great and striking fact of the preservation of the people of Beni-Israel, and its increase at an epoch when the populations of other countries were slowly dying out, is to be attributed solely to the curb which the law imposed on domestic slavery, and which it partially maintained even in the times of the greatest national decay.

On our knowledge of the internal organism and economy of the Hebrews, may be based certain deductions as to the domestic economy of other contemporaneous nations, especially those of Syria and certain parts of west Asia. Lydia, and above all, Babylon and Assyria are historically known only in the last stages of their existence, when political and domestic slavery had almost completely fused themselves together. For earlier times, the sources of investigation are limited, if not altogether wanting, and analogy alone can guide research. It is, however, probable that only the Mosaic law remained to combat and regulate serfdom and slavery with moral and legal weapons. The Hebrews did not possess, and did not transmit to history, any of the products of a brilliant civilization or of a refined culture such as reaches us in echoes from the antique oriental empires. But the Hebrews were, at the same time, endowed with certain spiritual impulses, aspirations and ideas, far grander than those of any of the surrounding nations. Material civilization and culture cannot be considered as the highest manifestation of man's spirit. History presents examples of the development of the noblest human impulses to a degree out of all proportion with the so-called "civilization" of the nation.

The authority of the Scriptures is invoked as absolute sanction for the enslavement of one branch of the human family; and the theological right to enslave the African is based on the well-known words of Noah: "Cursed be Canaan: a servant of servants shall he be unto his brethren." The general import of these words, however, even in the strictest construction, has rather a reference to their degradation as a caste–exemplified in the case of the swineherds among the Egyptians, or the Çudras (Soudras) among the Hindus–either of which, however, were chattels deprived of human and family rights.

Modern criticism, guided chiefly by the light of comparative philology and ethnology, has established beyond any doubt the genuine meaning of the patriarchal names of Scripture. Down to Abraham, or at the utmost to Terah his father, all those names bear an ethnical or geographical signification. Abraham, however, is an historical person, and with him positive Jewish history opens.

Moses and the other writers of the book of Genesis were educated among the highly learned and scientific Egyptians; and in Palestine they came in contact with a highly advanced civilization among the Canaanites or Phœnicians, Arabians, and Nabatheans, who were then in the full tide of life and action. From these kindred Shemitic peoples the Hebrews learned the use of written characters; and many of the scientific discoveries of these epochs are dimly preserved in the Mosaic record, as also the general outlines of the ethnic knowledge of the age. Moses and the other writers did but record the various geographic and ethnic names which came to their ears, and for this no inspiration was necessary. Modern scientific criticism, guided by the inductions of reason-that grandest product of the hand of God-now infuses living spirit into what was for ages a dead and incomprehensible letter. This can be easily elucidated by a few examples. The word Ham, or *Erez-Cham*, has no root or meaning in Hebrew or any other Shemitic dialect; it was doubtless borrowed from the Egyptians, and to Egypt must we go for the solution of its signification. Other Biblical names, as, for example, *Eber*, *Pheleg* or *Peleg*, *Reu* or *Rehu*, *Serug* and *Nahor*, represent distinct Shemitic tribes, or, as the record tropically styles them, kingdoms and states, of Mesopotamia (Naharaina). *Eber*, or more properly, *Heber* (whence our "Hebrews"), signifies "the stranger" or "a person from the other side," that is, one who came from a foreign region. *Aram* also implies an immigrant from the other side of the Euphrates. So, likewise *Misraim* (the *Misr* or M-R of the Egyptians), *Cush*, *Phut* and *Lud*, constituted distinct tribes and nations in widely distant regions, and perhaps even belonged to different races, according to accepted schemes of ethnology. *Lud* answers to the Libyan *Lewutub*, the *Leguatan* of the Byzantine writers, and the classical *Garaman*. *Phut* and *Lud* belong to Africa; they are brothers of Mizraim, or its nearest ethnic relations in the remotest antiquity, or perhaps closely allied but independent tribes-as the Scriptures generally record tribes and states politically and geographically independent. *Phut* and *Lud* are also mentioned as the allied troops of the Egyptians, or of the Syrians. Finally *Lud* (*Ludim*) descends from Mizraim; so it may be that they were a branch of the Egyptian stem, just as the Irish are an offshoot of the Gallo-Celtic stock, or the Anglo-Saxons of the Teutonic trunk.

The curse of Noah was hurled against *Canaan*. The philological and ethnic signification of this name has already been explained. The Canaanites, although themselves but an elder branch of the Shemitic family, were the enemies of Beni-Israel, who conquered them and drove them from their land and homes. There is thus a manifest logic in the writer of this part of Genesis condemning them to eternal servitude-for it was written after the subjugation of the Canaanites. Indeed, the same policy of enslavement was pursued by almost all the ancient conquering nations in the flush of their victorious battles; and so, in later times, did the Longobards of Italy, the Goths and Franks in Gaul and Spain, the Anglo-Saxons in Britain, and the Normans in England and Ireland.

There seems to be no scientific doubt that the cursed Canaanites were of the same family and stock as the Hebrews. After the most searching and conscientious investigations in ethnology and philology, it is impossible to regard the Canaanites or Phœnicians as other than Shemites; and with this also coincide the Scriptures-their land of Canaan is not in Africa. Who the *Cushites* of antiquity were, has likewise been already pointed out. And if, as some have attempted to prove, the ancient Egyptians were not of the African race (according to our modern designation), then they were the Chamites, Cushites, etc., of Scripture. How, through them, the curse can be shown to reach the genuine African, requires an effort of casuistry repulsive both to logic and fact-nay, to the baldest common sense. Not the dimmest shadow of authority can be tortured from the Scriptures for the enslavement of the black or negro race. With somewhat sounder logic has this curse of Canaan been applied, even in Christian times, and among European nations, to classes kept in bondage by masters belonging to the same race. Slavery, indeed, has been the common fate, in successive epochs, of all human races and families; and the oppressor has never been wanting in a pious plea. The so-called nobility of the mediæval Christian ages considered the burghers and subdued laborers as being of impure and degraded blood, and all over Europe they were held to be the descendants of Ham. (Some old aristocratic European families even now consider all who are not nobles to be of the degraded caste). According to this construction of the Noachic curse, the foul taint even now circulates not in the vein of the African slave, but in the veins of the tyrants who oppress him. Neither the Egyptians, Phœnicians, Hebrews, nor, indeed, any nation of antiquity, considered any special race or tribe as absolutely predestined to eternal bondage. This abominable conception is a putrid growth from mental, social and moral decay. Even Moses had a black woman for his wife (not his concubine), and, nevertheless, was admitted to converse with Jehovah.

The present historical investigation aims not at the vindication of the African: science and history do this triumphantly for all honest and intelligent minds. These pages have but in view to exhibit the terrific havoc and devastation which domestic slavery brings on all races, nations and civilizations, and to point out the complete analogy of slavery as it existed in the past with that which still blasts our country and our age. The leprosy of early Egypt, Syria and Judea, was the same as that which existed long centuries afterward in western Europe; and so also is it with the social leprosy of the ages. And as, in special conditions, a disease may assume a more deadly intensity, so also do social maladies at times show themselves with increased virulence. In antiquity, domestic slavery seized hold of all races and all social and civil conditions: it was not exclusively fastened on any special race. It may be for this reason that it ate but slowly into the marrow of the antique civilizations. Now modern sophistry attempts to give a divine and moral sanction to chattel slavery, and bases its justice on the absolute and predestined inferiority of the *black race*. But the natural work of slavery in destroying manhood, morals and intellect, progresses with terrible rapidity in this country, and is here receiving its most mournful illustration.

But what is the testimony of the highest scientific generalization on this question, of the natural inferiority of the African? All the authoritative names in comparative anatomy and physiology-Owen, Flourens, Bachman, Muller, Haenle, Pritchard, Wagner, Vogt and Draper, among them-together with men of the mental calibre and scientific attainments of William and Alexander von Humboldt-men of every variety of scientific theory, and discussing the question from every possible stand-point —universally deny the existence of any absolute inferiority of the negro race, or even any essential difference or line of demarcation between the races at all! The physiological and craniological differences which are so easily observed, do not amount to a difference of *species*; and cerebral physiology makes no essential distinction between the brain of a white man-even an Anglo-Saxon —and that of a negro.

Still more groundless are the current assertions concerning the mental inferiority of the African race. If such an inferiority really exists at the present day, it is, at the utmost, but transient and conditional in its nature. It can only be such an inferiority as for countless centuries characterized the northern races in contrast to the southern. While the former roved and fought as savages in the wilds and forests, the latter were elaborating grand and harmonious civilizations. It is difficult to imagine what would have been the condition of the Germans-aye, even of the Anglo-Saxons —what kind of civilization they would have inaugurated-without their Christian, Roman and Gallo-Celtic inoculation. If it be urged that certain African tribes *are* less susceptible of culture, or less endowed with intellectual qualities and capacities than certain white tribes or their offshoots-is it not also the case that the offspring from the same parents may have widely varying powers, tendencies and capacities; and that diverse tribes and nations springing from the same ethnic source, have played very different parts in the drama of universal history?

In the remotest antiquity, the great Gallo-Celtic stem actively influenced the destinies of Europe, and a part of Asia; yet it is only eighty years since the historian Pinckerton, speaking of *Ireland* and the *Irish* —those purest Celtic remains, said: "It is indeed a matter of supreme indifference at what time the savages of a continent peopled a neighboring island" (Ireland). This remark it would be difficult to justify-although there are even now many Englishmen who consider the genuine Irish an inferior race, and one, too, incapable of any high development.

The moral and mental growth of those Africans who were formerly slaves in the British West Indies, shows the possibility of negro culture under the influence of freedom. The official reports of the various governors of these islands, show that, since emancipation, there has been a rapid and steady growth of their prosperity; and the absolute veracity which characterizes these reports of English agents to their government cannot for a moment be doubted. In some of the islands, such as Nassau and others, the products and revenues have increased a hundred-fold, while the cost of administration (for keeping protective fleets and repressive soldiery, needed now no more) has greatly diminished. They also certify to a great increase in the imports from England-their mother country in the noblest sense of the word. Even the *export* of sugar is nearly equal to what it was under the forced labor of slavery, while *its intrinsic production has vastly increased* —the domestic consumption far surpassing what it was in the palmiest days of the planters. These are facts which only hypocrisy can pervert, or perversion conceal.

With reference also to the question of the "viability" and longevity of hybrids, mulattoes, etc., science protests against the fallacy which the new pro-slavery apostles advocate. Facts confirm the deductions of genuine science, and explode the fallacies of its counterfeit. The Dominican Republic is almost entirely composed of a mulatto population, which is now in its second or third generation, if not older. Neither are these mulattoes dying out, but they are increasing by and within themselves. No human white stallions are imported there from slave-breeding regions to correct or keep up the breed.

If, however, there should still linger a presumption of the superiority of the white over the black man, it must speedily vanish when the arguments of the militant upholders of slavery-whether they be in senatorial togas, in priestly robes, or in printer's ink-are subjected to the analysis of impartial philosophy or common logic. A spurious and depraved civilization is far more dangerous and degrading to society, and more truly evidences positive mental inferiority, than does the absence of civilization or the primitive savage condition. And this is the more true when the subjects of such a spurious civilization have within reach the elements of a genuine moral and social culture, but at the same time spurn and depreciate them all. Such persons, whatever may be their conventional position or ethnic descent, whatever the color of their skin, the form of their skull, or the nature of their hair, are singly and collectively inferior to the uncultivated and oppressed and hence degraded negro; while in respect of justice, manhood, and all that is ennobling, they make no approach to the millions of industrious and intelligent farmers and free yeomanry, artisans, and mechanics of the free states, still less with the higher manifestations of these qualities in great and generous minds.

Neither in the Mosaic record, therefore, nor the native sense of morality, still less in science, can any support be found for the fallacies propounded by the apostles of American slavery. Science, just and elevated in its intrinsic nature, deduces conclusions and establishes laws with sublime impartiality, extenuating naught, and setting down naught in malice. The normal character of every science, always and forever, is *emancipatory*. Science emancipates the mind from prejudices, falsehoods, and superstitions, and from the tyranny exercised over man by the elements and forces of nature, as well as from the far more malignant forces of social oppression. It is doubtless this divine character of true science which makes it so repulsive to the apostles of human degradation.

VI. Nabatheans

Lassen, Quatremère, Laborde, Oppert, Chwolsohn, Perceval, etc.

In the gray morning of time, behind the obscurity hovering over the origin of Assyria, and preceding even the first great epoch of Babylon, dawns the fully-developed Nabathean civilization. In proportion as scientific investigation imagines it has reached a positive epoch in the ethnology and history of our race, a new cloud ever rises behind it, which is but of this service-unerringly to indicate the limits of the space already investigated. Thus legends, traditions, and tracings sink helpless and hopeless into mythus, and the investigator is lost in the "dark backward and abysm of time." The Eastern legends hanging over Fore-Asia (or the lands between the Himalayas and Assyria), present traditions of epochs and civilizations which had traversed the periods of youth, maturity, and decline, before Brahmins, Assyrians, or Hebrews even dawned on the historical horizon.

The Nabatheans are supposed to have been Shemites or pure Chaldeans.[9] They dwelt in ancient Mesopotamia, between the Euphrates and the Tigris, and also in what afterward constituted a part of Syria and Assyria; and their branches or colonies extended to Arabia and to eastern Mesopotamia. They were probably the primitive white dwellers in these regions, and the founders of Babylon and of her first-almost pre-historic —epoch of glory, down to the time when they were conquered by the Assyrians or by Aryanized Nabatheans and Chaldeans.

According to ancient eastern writers, they invented and taught to their neighbors the art of tilling the soil, and from this circumstance they are said to have derived their name. At all events they were the primitive cultivators of these lands, and agriculture seems to have been their principal pursuit and mode of livelihood. This highly-flourishing Nabathean civilization underlaid the Assyrian and second Babylonian civilizations, and powerfully influenced the primitive Hebrew writers. *Arphaxad*, mentioned in Genesis, signifies in Chaldaic, *stronghold, city, civilization*, and this, too, at the earliest so-called patriarchal epoch. To the Nabatheans belongs the great work of irrigating Euphratia, by which these heretofore barren and uncultivated plains were made, for more than forty centuries, the most fertile region of the ancient world. It is asserted, too, by the oldest authorities, that their language was highly developed at a time when the other Shemitic tribes and nations only lisped their rude tongue, or attempted to spell the symbols invented, in all probability, by the Nabatheans. Some attribute to them the invention of the arrow-headed characters, while others suppose that the Assyrians (of whom hereafter), first devised them, or at all events, first applied this Tartar invention for the use and preservation of the Nabathean language. Fragments from the writings of Kouthai —a Nabathean, who lived long before the destruction of Nineveh-show that most of the sciences, such as mathematics, astronomy, chronology, etc., were cultivated by them to a high degree, and that they were great lovers of music and other fine arts.

Their historical records are far richer and more complete than any other existing records which relate to those distant and as yet all but incomprehensible epochs and events. In these relics many details of the early life of that time are embodied, principally relating, however, to agriculture, and from which, doubtless, the Greek writers, as Dionysius of Halicarnassus, and Strabo, derived their knowledge of the superiority and paramount importance of Nabathean agricultural science, on which, as already remarked, their whole civilization was based. Nowhere, however, in these venerable Nabathean fragments is *slavery* or the *slave* ever mentioned, and still less as constituting the basis of domestic husbandry and field labor; but *freemen* and *freeholders* only are alluded to as cultivating the land and reaping the rewards of their toil; thus furnishing an additional and most forcible proof that human *slavery is not coeval with the existence of society*.

Indeed, it may be stated as a general rule, clearly confirmed by history, that agriculture never can flourish under slave labor, nor even under villanage. It never did so in antiquity and it never has done so in modern times. In proportion as Egypt, Syria and Assyria fell a prey to political servitude and her twin-sister, or rather generator, domestic slavery, did their agriculture deteriorate and decay. In proportion as the nations of modern Europe have emerged from slavery and serfdom, has agriculture become a civilizing agency, progressive, rational and scientific. England, Germany, France, Switzerland, Belgium and Flanders, are living witnesses thereof; and, on the other side, Poland, Russia, Hungary, Bulgaria, and the Danubian Principalities-all possessed of the most fertile soils-scarce emerge from social, political and rural barbarity. The Moors and the Moriscoes were not slaves when they cultivated Andalusia in a manner never equalled. And what a wide difference between the agriculture of the free and slave sections of the United States! and that too, though the region of slave culture enjoys advantages both in climate and soil. The halting and uncertain advances made in the slave country, are but dimly breaking rays from the free, enlightened northern states.

Thus do the oldest and the newest teach one lesson and tend to one result.

VII. Assyrians and Babylonians

AUTHORITIES:

Rawlinson, Duncker, Oppert, M. von Niebuhr, etc.

The mighty empire of the Assyrians, which constitutes one of the first links in the chain of positive history, has hitherto been best known by the great catastrophes which finally closed its existence. The Hebrew Scriptures testify to the wealth, the luxury, and the military power of the Assyrians; but neither these nor the fragments in other ancient historical writers, dispel the obscurity enveloping the interior organism of that great antique people. Neither do the outlines of Babylonian history given by Herodotus afford much insight into the details of her social structure.

In that fore-world which history has not yet penetrated, the region between the Mediterranean sea and the head-waters and affluents of the Euphrates and the Tigris, formed the theatre of a tumultuous confusion of races, nations and civilizations, which has no parallel in the known history of mankind. Social and ethnic structures of the most heterogeneous kind covered those regions, with their various creeds, theocracies, municipalities monarchies and despotisms of every degree.

When, about fifteen centuries B.C., history unveils the empire of the Assyrians or Ninevites, their dominion extended in a direct line from the head-waters of the Euphrates and Tigris to the mouths of those rivers; on the north-east, also, they ruled over Media (thus touching the Caspian), and from thence their dominion stretched across Armenia, southern Caucasus and Georgia, westward to the mouth of the river Halys (the modern Kizil-Ermak), in the Black Sea, and embraced also Palestine, Phœnicia and Kilikia. As the dynasty of Ninus once ruled over Lydia, it is probable that the Ninevite empire at one time extended over at least a part of Asia Minor, as far as the Egean Sea.

This great Assyrian empire rose on the ruins of Babylon, which was once her master, and which was also far superior to her in antiquity.

History has preserved the names of some of the races and tribes which may here at one time have dwelt side by side, but which were subsequently conquered and ruled by the more powerful nation. History, we say, has preserved some, and comparative philology is constantly disentangling others from the chaos of antique Mesopotamian ethnology.[10]

The Assyrian and Babylonian empires stand recorded in the history of humanity as having been the cradles of Eastern despotism and political slavery. How this terrible tyranny arose in Assyria there are no means of ascertaining. Doubtless there were a number of conspiring causes, just as many rills unite to form a powerful stream. In the history of Rome, fortunately we shall be able clearly to seize the genesis of her despotism, and exhibit the germ as well as the wreck of her social structure. Reasoning from all historic analogy, however, it may safely be asserted that Assyrian despotism was generated by war, while political bondage nursed and fostered domestic chattelhood. Evil ever reproducing its own substance and shadow!

The social and domestic economy of the Assyrians must, in its general features, have been similar to that of the Nabatheans and Hebrews. In the course of time, domestic slavery may, to some extent, have been developed in both empires; but even in the last stages of their independent existence, it could not have reached that terrible point it attained after the loss of their autonomy. Assyria and Babylon fell by the blows of nations who were themselves subdued and politically enslaved. To the last, however, neither their lands nor cities were ever devastated or desolated. Their civilization remained in a flourishing condition to the last, and historically it stands as *original*. But original civilizations are never germinated under the influence of domestic chattelhood. The plains of the Euphrates must have been the hive of a rural population whence the imperial armies were supplied, and these supplies could not have been in the form of chattels. In ancient cities, manufactures and industry were often carried on by slaves; but when domestic slavery established itself in the rural regions, the national forces soon became palsied.

The tribes and countries conquered by Assyria and Babylon were simply made tributary to their wealth and power. Prisoners of war were, in all likelihood, disposed of in the same manner as they were in Egypt, and as was the custom all over the ancient world, and indeed, for several centuries in Christendom-employed in the public works, in the cutting of those canals whose traces are still visible, or in raising walls, palaces and public edifices, all of which are now covered mountain high with the dust of ages. Thus Sargon (or Sargina), for example, employed prisoners of war in constructing the vast palaces of Khorsabad.

Assyrian and Babylonian history records repeated transportations of whole populations from one part of the empire to another. The condition of such captives on becoming colonists has already been explained in the section upon the "Hebrews." It would seem that the kings of Assyria and Babylon first inaugurated this mode of wholesale transportation, captivity and colonization. Thus Tiglath-Palassar deported the inhabitants of Damascus to Kur in Georgia; and Assardan sent off, *en masse*, Babylonians, Arkeans, Susianians, Elamites, Persians and Daheans (Tartars), some north and others south. All such transplantments begot destruction, desolation and the breaking up of homesteads; and thus fostered domestic slavery, facilitated its expansion, and increased its fatal influence over both the conquered and the conquerors. And finally, they prepared the soil for that poisonously luxuriant growth of slavery by which Mesopotamians and Syrians became the general bondmen of classical antiquity.

After the destruction of the Assyrian capital (Nineveh) by the revolted nations, Babylon became the centre of a new empire. The rule of Nabukudrussur (a Chaldean from Babylon), extended from the mountains of Armenia to the Arabian shores of the Red Sea, and to the Persian Gulf. This again is a record of perpetual war, and was, in all respects, a continuation of the Ninevitian period of desolation and captivity. Prisoners of war again filled the capital, and worked at the walls and palaces of Babylon. The rich valleys were no longer cultivated by free laborers, but were in the hands of large slaveholders, and tilled by their gangs of slaves.

Babylon fell, destroyed by war, combined with political and domestic slaveries, and she transmitted both diseases to her destroyers.

VIII. Medes and Persians

AUTHORITIES:

Zend Avesta, Vendidad, Herodotus, Lassen, Pictet, Duncker, etc.

The Medes and Persians, or Zend-speaking Iranians, those destroyers of the Assyrian and Baby-lonian empires, were a mighty branch of the great family of Aryas. The Iranians left the common home of the Aryas at a period so distant as to render useless every effort toward giving it possible or even probable chronology. They settled in regions called by them "Lands of Iran," which, up to the present day, constitute Persia. Some investigators assert that Iran-Persia was previously occupied by Tartars; but the earliest traditions preserved in the Zend, or ancient speech of Zarathustra, do not mention any struggles for supremacy between the races as having taken place.

The Zend Avesta, the oldest traditional record of the people of Iran, presents a picture of the primitive migrations and the social condition of the Iranians. It exhibits them as divided into three classes-priests, soldiers and farmers; though, as yet, there was no such thing as the circumscription of caste. It would seem that the fusion with the Tartars-the supposed aborigines of Iran-was complete, as the Zend Avesta makes no mention of any subjugated people or lower class. The warriors and the agriculturists stood on a perfect social equality. The book of tradition nowhere mentions serfdom, slavery, or property in man. This would seem to authorize the conclusion that among the early Iranians, property in man was unknown. Certainly, at all events, if even the forms of slavery were present, they were in such abeyance as to escape the attention of Zarathustra (Zoroaster), the great moralist and lawgiver of his people, who lived long after the epoch of the early wanderings, and when the Iranic nation formed a well-organized society on Iran's soil. Zarathustra considers agriculture as morally and socially the noblest human occupation; but he speaks of the generous labor of freemen, not the forced drudgery of slaves.

The Vendidad contains frequent allusions to the general occupations of life, and is especially minute regarding the details of husbandry-its wants, modes, products and implements. The farmer is to have at least a team of draught cattle, a harness and a whip; a plough, a hand-mill, and so forth; but there is no mention whatever of a slave as an agricultural requisite. The homestead of an Iranian consists of a habitation, a storehouse, a cellar, stables for horses, camels and cattle; but the records have no allusion to a cabin for the slaves. The Vendidad also describes how dogs-almost sacred to the Iranians-are to be posted to watch over the village and the herds; but nowhere says that they were to be used for watching and hunting slaves. Various operatives and artisans are enumerated, but none of them as bond-servants or as working under compulsion.

The farmers, peasants and operatives of Media and Persia-so admired even by Xenophon and Plato-thus built up a vigorous state and society. After long centuries of existence, however, its strength was undermined by foreign conquests, by luxury, and by political and domestic slavery. A similar phenomenon will present itself again and again in the course of this investigation. When the Medes overthrew the Assyrian empire, they became infected with the dissolute customs of their former masters. The houses of the wealthier were filled with domestic slaves; though, as yet, slavery did not come in contact with agriculture or the industrial pursuits, and so spread like a blight over the land.

Domestic slavery, in the limited sense of household servitude, was doubtless ultimately introduced into Persia; but never was Persian held as *chattel* on his ancestral soil. Nor yet did despotism, or political slavery, exist in the governmental structure of the Iranians, who, led by Kyros (Cyrus), conquered the whole western Asiatic world. Kyros was only the first among his peers, and was all-powerful only as a leader and commander. He had not yet the despotic power of Xerxes and other and later scions of the Achæmenides; and to the last, even to the conquests by Alexander, the Iranic social structure was comparatively free from domestic slavery. Nor were the Persians and other Iranian tribes ever the absolute political slaves of their own kings.

The Persian conquerors of the Asiatic world found domestic slavery more or less developed wherever they penetrated. Positive information, however, is extremely scanty regarding the special social and political organization of the Persians after Kyros and under Dareios. The rule of the Achæmenides extended over about eighty millions of men, belonging to various races. The conquerors, in all cases, respected the civil and social organization and administration peculiar to the subjugated tribes or nations. In numerous instances, the sovereigns of conquered states became Persian satraps over lands they once ruled in their own right. As satraps they were possessed of oppressive authority, had the power of life and death, of forcing exactions and levying taxes. But, as the Persian kings were, to the last, strict observers of Zarathustra's precepts, agriculture always continued to be the most favored pursuit. The satraps were rewarded with strict reference to the degree in which agriculture flourished and the population grew and prospered in their respective satrapies.

During the long rule of the descendants of Dareios, comparative peace prevailed in the interior of the great empire, which swept from the Nile almost to the Indus. So that domestic slavery did not find its usual supplies from prisoners of war, or by the destruction of small properties and consequent domestic impoverishment-those terrible sequels of wars from which Fore-Asia had suffered almost uninterruptedly for many previous centuries.

For these and other reasons, domestic slavery under the Persian rule, although sheltered by political servitude, had but small growth and made but slow progress. It certainly did not desolate the lands with the blight and barrenness that afterward depopulated them under Roman rule.

The tribute paid by the subdued nations to the Persian kings and their court, included slaves-boys and girls-but in a limited number. The slave-traffic existed as of old; but, in all probability, the supply of the human merchandise was less plentiful. From political slaves, but not domestic chattels, it was that the armies were recruited which crossed the Hellespont and invaded Greece.

But, viewing the matter in the gross and scope of historical development, political slavery and the blighting effects of the oppressive despotism to which the Persians were long subjected, may be looked upon as the soil out of which grew the morbid and monstrous system of domestic slavery, just as external influences frequently develop and foster the germs of a chronic and fatal bodily disease.

IX. Aryas-Hindus

AUTHORITIES:

Lassen, Wilson, Weber, Max Müller, Pictet, Kuhn, etc.

The central region of Baktria was in all probability the cradle of the Aryas, the common progenitors of all the races and nations which now cover Europe. In times anterior to the great pre-historic division and separation of the Aryan races, they probably occupied the whole of the vast region stretching from the Hindu-Kush, the Belourtagh, to the river Oxus and the Caspian Sea. This, too, at a period of which it can only be said that time existed.

The antique Aryas led a pastoral life. The original signification of the words in the European languages denoting family and social relations, as well as the names of domestic and other animals, of grains and plants, of implements of husbandry and handicraft and the like, is elucidated by roots found in Sanscrit, which is supposed to have been the original language of the Aryas, or, at any rate, the one which most completely preserved the primitive impress of the Aryan character.

"Father" (in Sanscrit, *pitri*), signifies "the protecting one, or the protector;" "mother" (Sanscrit, *matri*), "she who regulates or sets in order;" "daughter" (*duhitri*), "the milking one;" "son" (*sunu*), "the begotten;" "sister" (*vastri*), "she who takes care," —subauditur, of household matters-also, "the bearer of a new family;" "brother" (*brhatri*), "the helper, or carrier;" "youth" (*yavan*) "the defender." So also, "horse" (*açva*), signifies "swift, rapid;"[11] the name for the "bovine" genus, bull and cow (Sc., *go, gaus*), "to sound inarticulately," likewise (*ukshan*) "fecundating," besides other names with other significations; the "ovine" genus, or sheep kind (*avi*), implies "the loved, protected," etc.; the "dog" (*'cvan, kvan*), means "the yelper, barker;" but he has also other names denoting his qualities, as *sucaka*, "spy, informer," *krtagna*, the "recognizing," or "grateful one," etc.; "goose," (*hansa*, from Sc. *has*), "to laugh." So the roots for the general names of grains and fruits are to be found in the Sanscrit; thus, *ad*, "to eat;" *adas*, "nourishment;" *gr*, "to devour," whence *garitra*, "grain," "rice," etc. It may be noticed that derivatives from these and other roots became applied, in branch languages, to various special kinds of grain; thus, "oats," both in form and signification, is easily traced to a Sanscrit root. So, too, the names of many metals, trees, plants and wild animals, have their roots and descriptive meaning in the Aryan or Sanscrit language; and comparative philology gives us the method of seizing the affiliations of form and of meaning.

Words of the character pointed one and their primitive significations-constituting the foundation of man's family and social existence-followed the various ethnic branches issuing from the Aryan and expanding over the ancient world. *But no root, no name, no signification is to be found for a "servant" bearing the meaning of "slave" or "chattel,"* or expressive of a deprivation of the rights of manhood or of human dignity. The primitive Aryan mode of life was naturally patriarchal or clan-like, and the above-mentioned words show that household and rural functions were performed by the members of the family. What has been already said in another division (see "Hebrews"), applies even more forcibly to the Aryas. The Sanscrit word *ibha*, signified "family," "household," "servants," but *never slaves or chattels*. Both its sound and sense are still perfectly preserved in the Irish *ibh*, which signifies "country," or "clan;" *not enslaved men*! The names of weapons, and other words relating to warfare, which may be traced back to the Aryan speech, prove that the Aryas warred with other tribes-perhaps with the Tartars; and all such foreign enemies were comprehended under the collective Sanscrit denomination of *barbara, varvara,* or "barbarians." But even here, where we should most look for it, no hint or trace of slavery can be found.

The attempt, historically, to endow certain human families or races with special fitness or capacity for freedom or slavery-or with a fatality toward the one or the other, or toward certain fixed social and political conditions-as well as the effort to divide the human family into distinct physiological or psychological races-all manifests a narrow appreciation of the course of human events; it evidences a very limited knowledge of positive history, and perhaps a still more limited philosophical comprehension of its spirit. If, however, such classifications had any scientific basis, assuredly the Aryas and the nations issuing from them had no natural, special propensity either to be slaves or slave-makers.

It win be hereafter pointed out, that among the various branches of the Aryas, or what are called Indo-Europeans, slavery was not a feature of their primitive life, but was the result of a long subsequent epoch of moral decay and degradation. It was at a comparatively late period of their history and under precisely the same conditions, that the Romans and Greeks began to enslave their own fellows. So was it with the Gaels or Celts, and so also with the Slavi. The Poles were free from serfdom till the thirteenth Christian century; the Russians only introduced it toward the close of the sixteenth-and in both cases after dissension, war, and desolation. The Teutons alone (Anglo-Saxons included), seen in the light of primitive history, had slavery in their household and in their national organism, and the slaves, too, of their own race and kin.

The Aryas descended the slopes of Hindu-Kush and the Himalayas, entering the region of the Five or of the Seven Rivers (Punjab), wandered along the river Jamuna, on the line between Attock and Delhi, successively spread over the whole region between the Indus and the Ganges-and here begins their historical existence as a people. In the course of this long march they conquered or drove before them-seemingly without any great trouble, at least in the first encounters, the aboriginal occupants of the Trans-Himalayan countries; and this, too, before they reached what may be called the threshold of history. Discords and wars early broke out among them, principally caused by the continual pressure of northern immigrants upon the possessors of the fertile countries in the south-caused, too, by the struggles for supremacy between families or dynasties, when the tents of the patriarchs had expanded into populous tribes, and almost into nations; and also by the struggles of classes created in the effort to subjugate the aboriginal inhabitants, especially those in the southern parts of India. All these wars took place at a very early epoch, and elude positive chronological division. Their history, as well as that of the primitive Aryan or Hindu mode of life, and their earliest spiritual conceptions, are pictured in the Vedas, which form the background of the whole Indian world.

The gray and venerable Vedaic age is now divided by critics into four periods: the Chhandas period, the Mantra period, the Brahmana period, and the Sutra period.

The Chhandas period exhibits the purest patriarchal and peaceful condition of the family. There were then no priests and no division of classes; the father offered up simple sacrifices to heaven, and the simple hymns and songs of the family resounded over the offering. If the household contained any captive of the aboriginal race, such a one, by renouncing his ancient customs and creed, and accepting the language, the faith and the law of the conqueror, retained life and comparative liberty. And, moreover, all ethnological investigations confirm the belief that the aborigines of India were of the negro, or what is commonly called African family. On this American continent the kidnapped and enslaved African has accepted both the creed and the language of his oppressor-but for him there is neither liberty nor law.

Not to enslave, but only to subdue-preserving, at least partially, the rights of the conquered-was the policy of the Aryas in their encounter with barbarians. And in the domestic wars of tribes and dynasties which yet dimly echo through the second or Mantra period, no traces of the enslavement of their conquered enemies are to be found. In general, the first two periods not only do not show any shadow of *slavery* in the domestic and social relations, but even the division into *classes* or *castes* does not yet make its appearance. During the third or Brahmana period, the Vedas give an account of the terrible and bloody struggle which ended in the social and religious victory of the Brahmas, or Brahmins, over the Kshatriyas, who had previously formed the ruling families.

The Brahmins now reorganized the religious and political structure of the Hindus. They divided society into four classes or castes: (it is to be noted here, however, that some modern exegetists assert that the true meaning of the Sanscrit word *Varna*, for "caste," is not yet clearly apprehended). These four castes were: 1. The Brahmins; 2. The Kshatriyas; 3. The Vaisyas; 4. The Soudras, or Çudras. The first three correspond to the classification already mentioned as existing among the Iranians. The Çudras were the lowest and most degraded caste; still they were not enslaved, not the property of any other caste, not even of the Brahmins-those spiritual and political chiefs of the Hindus. The labors of agriculture ennobled even the hands of the Brahmin, and could not be performed by slaves nor under the compulsory terrors of a master or driver.

As the word Çudras is not Sanscrit, it is supposed that it was the ethnic name of the sub-dued aborigines of which the fourth caste was composed. The offspring of a Brahmin and a Çudra was considered of pure blood. The Brahminic law authorized the enslavement of persons belonging to all the interior castes, for debt. Slaves may also have been made in the wars with the southward retreating aborigines and others; and slaves may occasionally have been sold in the markets, but their number must have been very insignificant. Laws for the servitude of the Çudras-if such existed even-must very soon have fallen into disuse; for when Alexander brought Greece and Europe into contact with India, the astonished Greeks found scarcely any slavery then existing. Several of the Greek authors even assert that a positive law prohibited any kind of enslavement.

Budha, the great precursor of the Christ, was moved to tears, affected to inspiration, by the suffering and oppression which resulted from the division of society into castes, and by the misery of the poor, who were oppressed by the rich land-owner; but among the social and moral plagues, Budha and his disciples enumerate not human slavery. As far as the history of antiquity is known, Budha was the first whose religious teaching broke through the narrow conception of nationality, and taught universal emancipation and the brotherhood of all tribes and nations of men.

The oppression of the poor and of the landless, which then existed in India, exists there still. It was strengthened by the terrible Mahomedan and Mongol conquests, and by the iron rule of the British East India Company. But the imposition by the Mahomedans and Mongols of an oriental despotism over the Hindus did not implant domestic chattelhood, nor did the English tax-gatherers ever cause Hindu humanity to be exposed for sale in the markets or bazaars.

X. Chinese

AUTHORITIES:

The Biots, Kaeuffer, Gutzlaff, etc.

China belongs to the present and to the remotest past of the Asiatic world. The historical existence of China and her civilization are at least coeval with that of Egypt and of Assyria, perhaps older than that of the Aryas.

Some geological investigators affirm that the table-land inclosed between the northern slopes of the Himalayas, the Kuenlun, the desert of Gobi-which is said to be older than the formation of the Himalayas-the Heavenly or Blue mountains, and the Altaï, was the first land which rose from the waters, and that therefore it was the first, and perhaps the only place in the north, where man appeared. This admitted, the probability is, that from that first human family issued a race bearing to-day various appellations, as the Yellow, the Altaïc, Turanian, Scythic, Finnic, Mongolian and Tartar-which is the last general denomination adopted by science, at least for the branches occupying central Asia, and reaching to the frontiers of Europe and the descendants of the Aryas. The first immigrants to China from the Kuenlun probably followed the current of the Yellow river; and it seems that the aborigines retired before the invaders, or perhaps the new yellow settlers mixed with the primitive occupants. In the southern parts of China, in the mountains of the interior, are still found tribes of dark-colored men resembling the negroes or the Pacific islanders, and using notched characters similar to those used by the Malays.

Agriculture seems to have been the sacred occupation of these yellow-hued settlers along the banks of the Yellow river-as it was in the valley of the Nile, of the Euphrates, and on the plains of Iran. Everywhere the origin of agriculture is lost in the night of time, and Quain or Cain-that is, the kernel, the young, the generating, etc., the husbandman of the Scriptures-is many thousand years older than Abraham, the wandering and slave-holding patriarch. The oldest Chinese records show agriculture to have been the special occupation of the father of a family, of the chief of a clan, and then of the emperor of the entire nation. With his own hands he directs the plough-therefore the plough could not have been desecrated by the hands of a slave. And it was not. In the family, in the domestic as well as in the national life, slavery first dimly appears only about the thirteenth century B.C.

In the remotest time, labor was, as it is now, the basis, the cement and the soul of the Chinese social and political life and growth-and by labor I mean, intellectual and manual labor in its most varied departments and developments. No classes, no castes, existed in the old primitive times; and perhaps, during many thousand years, no dynasties. The best and ablest person was selected as the chief and ruler: all the offices or functions were obtained by intellectual faculty and by superiority of knowledge, but not inherited; and the same system prevailed throughout all the occupations and pursuits of life. No labor whatever was degraded or degrading; it was carried on by men free and equal, and in principle recognized as such.

In China, as everywhere else, slavery appeared as a disease in the social body. It was generated by war and crime. Prisoners of war and condemned criminals became, so to say, slaves of the state, which used them for public labors or hired them out to private individuals. The highest officers of state, persons over seventy years old, and children, could not be condemned to slavery, excepting children exposed or abandoned by their parents. Slaves hired by private individuals were only used as helps or servants in households and families. But most of the servants were always freemen-they are so now; and slaves never were used in agriculture or in the different handicrafts. The land being generally considered as the property of the state, or of the emperor, the sovereign divided, distributed it, under certain conditions and servitudes, for tribute in money or kind, etc. But slaves are not mentioned among the various objects enumerated as constituting the tribute. The increase of population generated poverty, and paupers sold and still sell themselves or their children into slavery. Repeated domestic or internecine wars, recorded at a very distant historical epoch, were among the prominent agencies in increasing poverty. Impoverished persons and those deprived of their homes either sold themselves or became serfs attached to the soil, but not chattels. As serfs their legal condition and denomination is preserved in the books written about the twelfth century B.C., by Ma-tuan-lin—they are named *usurped families* or *usurpees*. Even after the conquest by the Mantschou Tartars, chattelhood did not get hold of the political structure, nor did it absorb the agricultural and industrial domestic economy of the Chinese. With the exception of the reigning family, no social position or function is privileged as hereditary; and in the same way, accidental slavery was not transmitted to the children of the enslaved. Their condition was and is controlled and regulated by law, which watches over the property of the state. Among the numerous domestic wars there are never recorded any revolts of slaves-an evidence of their very limited number.

Over-population generated and generates the most terrible and varied oppressions and miseries; but all of them lose their sting when compared with chattelhood. Over-population and misery generated the so-called coolie-system, which in principle is based on voluntary indenture. The reckless cruelties and the numerous infamies characterizing the manner in which the coolie trade is carried on, is evidence of the utter moral degradation and depravity of the white civilized Christian traders, and the inefficiency of their respective governments.

The Chinese civilization is commonly looked down upon from the heights of narrow-minded presumption and ignorance. About three thousand years B.C., public schools existed in China, and a full scientific and material culture prevailed there. Chinese records (among them the Books of the Sehu Kings), going back, perhaps, as far as two thousand five hundred years B.C. —contain the most correct and detailed statistical accounts of tribute, and give most reliable geographical notions of China, and of the subdued and neighboring countries-notions superior in exactitude to all similar records transmitted from classical antiquity. The Chinese lived in houses, in orderly communities, were humanized, polished, familiar with the sciences, industries, and all kinds of refinements, at a time, and during countless centuries, when the races of northern Europe-prominently the Slavi, the Germans, the Anglo-Saxons included-did not, in all probability, even understand how to construct huts, and, as savages, roved about in the wilderness.

In a work written by Prince Tscheu-Kong, about one thousand one hundred years B.C., are given the most minute details of the then existing organization of the empire. The administrative mechanism of that distant epoch finds no equal in the whole history of governments or of nations. Several thousand years ago the empire was administered by six supreme state departments, each with perfectly defined attributes, each subdivided into special branches, with directors and all orders of lower officials and functionaries. Chinese civilization passed its periods of youth and maturity many thousand years ago; and its senility has not yet reached total decrepitude. It crumbles not to pieces even now in its comparatively disjointed and disorganized condition.

No one can consider China in any way a model social organism; but its duration is marvellous and unequalled in the history of the race. The absence of hereditary privilege and of chattelhood as social or religious institutions, accounts, among other reasons, for this unique phenomenon. With all its drawbacks and defects, this long-lived civilization, with its schools, its general intelligence, its thousands-of-years old routine, compares, in many respects, favorably with that in the Southern States calling itself Christian, which, having partly inherited the great European development, and receiving influences from the free sections of the Union, has, nevertheless, for the last thirty or forty years, turned on its own crooked tracks, and, now prohibits, under severe penalty, schools for the children of its field laborers, whom it keeps in bondage. It sighs also for a further extension of oligarchic privileges, and for the enslavement of all human labor: re-enslaves the free or expels them; legalizes and sanctifies the sum of all social villanies: whose last word is the Lynch law, and the reckless, lawless persecution of free speech and even of free thought; while assassination becomes more and more frequent.

In the most ancient Asiatic world, the primitive societies generally had analogous beginnings, whatever may have been the regions and climates cradling them, whatever the difference of time, epochs, or race-characteristics. Analogous events and conditions evoked similar developments in the primitive men. The manifestations of man's intellectual and physical activity were everywhere spontaneous: a transmission of the various rudiments of civilization cannot logically be admitted.

Osiris, Cain, Yao, were urged by like necessities, when they inaugurated agriculture in Egypt, in Euphratia, or along the valleys of the Yellow river. On the Nile, on the Euphrates, on the Ganges, on the Hoang-ho, man-red or black, white or yellow-observed nature, utilized even the inundations, regulated and embanked the beds of rivers, cut canals and trenches to irrigate the parched soil. Everywhere-and certainly without imitating each other-but urged by surrounding circumstances, man worked, toiled, constructed habitations with the materials at hand-stone in Egypt; bricks, plaster, wood, etc., in Babylonia and China; raised cities in rich and fertile plains, erected edifices, and invented characters and signs to fix and to transmit to others ideas, notions and facts. Whatever may have been the special nature and form of these characters, whether hieroglyphics or phonetics, etc., undoubtedly they were original and not transmitted creations. These inventions arose at places separated by distances then almost impassable, by the same necessities and thoughts, by observation and imitation of nature, and by many other inner and outer promptings and circumstances. The rudiments of mathematics, astronomy, and other sciences, were created by this contact of man's mind with nature; and it is difficult, if not impossible, to admit that Egyptians or Chaldeans were the instructors of the Aryas or of the Chinese, or *vice versa*.

Of late an attempt has been made to justify American chattelhood by the fact that at the birth of Christ, half of the population of the Roman empire-about sixty millions-groaned under domestic slavery. This estimate may be below the true mark; but the humanity whose emancipation or redemption was to be accomplished, was not limited to the Roman world. For, from Iran and the Indus to the Kuenlun ridges, dwelt a population five or six times greater than that which populated the Roman empire, and that, too, almost unvisited by that terrible social plague which is now represented as being a divine blessing. Whatever may have been the other multiform social calamities which befell them-wars, massacres, destructions, impoverishments, and desolations-are, after all, but transient visitations; while American chattelhood, as devised by its apostles, eternally degrades both master and chattel.

XI. Greeks

AUTHORITIES:

Polybius, Grote, O. Muller, Beckh, Curtius, Clinton, Finlay, etc.

At the foot of the Julian Alps, above the head of the Adriatic, the branch of the Aryas which peopled Greece separated from their brethren who wandered into Italy. Keeping to the coast of Adria, the seceders reached the mountainous gorges of Epirus and the plains of Thessaly. From the southern slopes of the Cambunian mountains and of Olympus, they, in course of time, spread over Greece and Peloponnesus. Such at least are the results of the most recent researches concerning the pioneers whose labors prepared that region for the part it afterward played in history. They cleared the forests, drained the marshes, cut canals to let out the stagnant waters in mountain-basins so common in Greece; they regulated the currents of rivers and streams, made the soil arable, and the region fit for man and for further culture. These primitive cultivators of the valleys of Greece, and builders of the Cyclopean structures, called themselves, or were called by others, *Pelasgi* (that is, *those issuing from black soil, etc.*), and are regarded as the earliest occupants of Hellenic soil. They were the first settlers, and most probably offshoots of the same original stem whose successive branches mingled with the Pelasgi, or crowded them out and took their place in history as Achives, Hellenes, and Ionians-the last being considered been ancient as well as by modern writers as having been the autochthones of Attica and of other neighboring regions. To these Pelasgi and other primitive occupants, to their laborious pursuits and occupations, to their simple social structure, as well as to the essentially primitive social life of the Greeks, Herodotus refers-asserting that at the outset slavery was unknown in Greece, and especially in Attica.

The Pelasgian epoch was succeeded by what is commonly called the legendary or heroic age. In this Homeric epoch free yeomen or agriculturists own and till the soil; all the handicrafts and professions are free. Carpenters, smiths, leather-dressers, etc., were all freemen, and so also were the bards and "the leeches" (a highly esteemed class in primitive Greece). But wealth already began to accumulate, and the farms of the more fortunate were tilled by poor hired freemen called Thetes.

The geographical conformation of Greece furnished, as it still does, a natural incitement to war and piracy. Both formed prominent characteristics of the heroic times. Phœnician vessels visited the shores, and Phœnician settlements and factories were built at various points. These traffickers, perhaps, taught the Greeks that the feeble may be profitably enslaved by the strong, or at any rate they were the customers of the Greek pirate.

The general Greek word for slave explains the origin of slavery. *Dmoos* and *dmoe*, slave, go back to *dmao* or *damao*, to subdue, to subjugate, and so bear witness of war and violence either between individuals, or between clans, tribes, and districts, and then of incursions into distant lands. Slavery became an object of luxury, but not of social and economical necessity. It was confined to the dwelling of the chiefs and the sovereign; but did not invade the whole community. Leaders of freebooting expeditions seized every kind of booty, taking as many prisoners as they could on sea and on land. If the expedition or foray failed, the chief and his followers became, in their turn, prisoners and slaves. The prisoners were employed for domestic use within the precincts of the dwelling, as servants, shepherds, etc., or were sold or exchanged for others. The Phœnicians sold Asiatics or Libyans to Greeks and to Pontian barbarians, and received in exchange the prey made by Greeks in Greece or in Pontus. The Phœnicians occasionally kidnapped women and boys and sold them to Asiatics, Africans, and Celt-Iberians. Then, as everywhere throughout remotest and classical antiquity, many of the enslaved had previously belonged to the higher and even the highest conditions in their respective tribes, nations, or communities. So Eumæus, the swineherd of Ulysses immortalized by Homer, was the son of a chief of some island or district, who, having been kidnapped by Phœnicians, was sold to Laertes. In mediæval times, likewise, the prisoner taken on the battle-field and kept for ransom, if not for service, often was superior in birth and station to his keeper. No such social classifications, however, are intrinsic or normal, but only conditional, relative, and conventional, even when inherited. Logically they have the same signification and value in a well-graduated society, with its castles, palaces, charters and other privileges, as on plantations or among roving nomads and savage tribes. And thus, among the Southern slaves, descending from prisoners of war or from kidnapped Africans, there may be several of a purer aristocratic lineage than many of their drivers, even if the latter were F.F.V.

Enfranchisement, manumission, and ransom were largely practised in legendary Greece. The children of freemen by slave-women were free, and equal to those of legitimate birth. Most of the wars and expeditions during the heroic or Achivian piratical epoch, were made for the sake of kidnapping men and women, to sell or to exchange with the Phœnicians for various luxuries. Such was the general origin of slavery at the time when history throws its first rays on the Grecian world.

Many defend slavery on the plea that it softened and softens the results of wars and inroads; that prisoners, once slaughtered, are preserved for the sake of being sold into slavery. But already, during the so-called heroic age of Greece, wars and forays were made for the express purpose of getting captives or for kidnapping. The robber or pirate was always sure to find a buyer for his booty, otherwise he would have had no inducement to act. And thus slavery, instead of softening war, was its very source. The Greeks of the heroic age were incited to make inroads and depredations by the facility and security they had of profitably disposing of their captives by selling them into slavery. The bloody drama played, many, many centuries ago, in Peloponnesus and Greece, on the Ionian and Egean seas, and among the islands of the Archipelago, is repeated to-day on both sides of the Atlantic-on African and on American shores and islands. The tribes in Africa war with each other, destroy and burn towns and villages, expressly and exclusively because they find customers for slaves among Christians, and among self-styled civilized, humanized white men. Thus much for the assertion that American slavery contributes to soften the fate of prisoners of war in Africa, and humanizes the savages. It bestializes them, together with their piratical purchasers and their Southern patrons. The analogy holds good here, at a distance of many thousand years and many thousand miles, among different social conditions, in a different civilization, and in the higher moral development of the white man.

New invasions successively rolled over the valleys of Hellas; they changed considerably the social condition of the populations, expelling or subduing many of the former occupants and yeomen. From the north, from Thessaly, poured Hellenes, Heraclides, and Dorians, west and south, principally into the Peloponnesus. Henceforth the whole Greek family was represented in history by two cardinal social, political, and intellectual currents, through the so-called Doric and Ionic races.

In Thessaly, serfdom-but not chattelhood-seems to have been anciently established. Newcomers subdued the earlier tillers of the soil. The subdued became *villeins*, bondsmen, *adscripti glebæ*. Such dependent cultivators were the Thessalian Penestæ, who paid over to the landowners a certain proportion of the produce of the soil; furnished those retainers by which the families of the chiefs, or the more powerful, were surrounded, and served in war as their followers. But they could not be sold out of the country; they had a permanent tenure in the soil, and enjoyed family and village relations. Perhaps more than twenty centuries afterward, this was also the condition of the rustics all over western and mediæval Europe, and in some parts this condition even lasted down to our century-everywhere similar events generating emphatically analogous results and conditions. The holdings of the Thessalian Penestæ were protected by the state, whose subjects they were, and not chattels of the individual proprietors. The Thessalian and Doric invaders and conquerors imposed a similar yoke wherever they were victorious and finally settled. The last Doric and Heraclidic invasion, which culminated in the institutions and history of Sparta, subdued the former occupants of Peloponnesus, some of whom were likewise of Doric origin. Of such origin, in considerable proportion, were the renowned Helots. So, also, in course of time, the descendants of the companions of Achilles became, in the north, serfs under certain conditions of a more liberal nature; while others, descending from the companions of Agamemnon and Menelaus, became Sparta's Helots.

The condition of the Helots, in many respects, was similar to that of the Penestæ of Thessaly. They could not be sold beyond the borders of the state, not even by the state itself, which apportioned them to citizens, reserving to itself the power of emancipation. They lived in the same villages which were once their own property, before conquest transformed the free yeomen or peasants into bondsmen. The state employed the Helots in the construction of public works. Their fate, however terrible it may have been, was altogether within the law, whereas other domestic slaves in Greece, just like those in the Southern States, depended upon the arbitrary will of individuals. The Spartan law had various provisions for the emancipation of the Helots. They served in the army and fought the great battles of the Lacedemonians. Will the South intrust their chattels with arms and drill them into military companies?

Sparta was the seat of an oligarchy, which owned the greater part of the lands of Laconia, and kept in dependency the other autochthonous tribes, which in some way or other escaped the fate of the Helots. Such were the Periokes, enjoying certain political and full civil rights. But, in the course of events, the oligarchy tried to violate those rights, and the Periokes joined Epaminondas against Sparta, facilitating its subjugation, just as, centuries afterward, they joined Flaminius and the Romans against their Spartan masters. In Lacedemonia, as in Attica, there existed small landholders, called *gamori* or *geomori*, and others called *autougroi* —rustics possessing petty patches of land, or farming small parcels owned by large proprietors. Just so in the South the large plantations are surrounded by poor whites, by "sand-hillers," etc., some of them owning small patches, generally of poorer soil; others altogether homeless and landless. Subsequently these *geomori*, etc. —poor, free populations and their homesteads-were almost wholly engulfed by large plantations and domestic slavery. This was the work of time, as in her great days scarcely any chattel was known in Sparta.

The landed oligarchy of our Southern plantations is in more than one respect analogous with that of Sparta. The city of Sparta itself was rather an agglomeration of spacious country habitations than resembling other great cities.

When the Dorians made Sparta the centre of their power, the lands of Laconia were divided into ten thousand equal lots for the ten thousand Spartan citizens. Undoubtedly the home-steads, cleared and owned by the first settlers and colonists in the South, were more equally divided than they are now; and the increase in the extent of plantations on the one hand, and the decrease of the respectability of the poorer settlers and their transformation into "poor oppressed white men,"[12] on the other, were both effected by domestic slavery. At the time of Lycurgus-about four hundred years after the division-the above number of oligarchs was reduced to nine thousand; at the time of Herodotus-about four hundred years after Lycurgus-to eight thousand; and thus a reduction of one-tenth took place during each period of from three hundred to four hundred years. This was the time of the world-renowned Spartan poverty and virtue. But wars, conquests, etc., changed the character of the Spartans; luxury and wealth crept in, and with them came large estates and domestic slaves, the latter chiefly consisting of Greek prisoners of war. At the beginning of the first Peloponnesian war, Sparta may have had two hundred and twenty thousand Helots, and there were comparatively few domestic slaves in that number. The Peloponnesian war made the Spartans leaders of Greece, but filled Sparta with prisoners from other Greek states, and introduced wealth: from that war begins the decline of the Spartan spirit. The Helots and the impoverished poor whites successively became chattels. Sparta could only muster seven hundred citizens against Epaminondas at Leuctra. During the period between Herodotus and Aristotle the number of citizens was reduced to little above one thousand. At the Macedonian conquest, Sparta averaged fourteen chattels for every three freemen. One hundred years after Aristotle, under King Agis, about two hundred oligarchs constituting the body politic, the citizens of Sparta owned nearly all the lands of Laconia, and worked them by chattels.

This numerical reduction of citizens and deterioration of their historic character principally affected the military standing of Sparta. Causes so obvious as not to require explanation prevent at present a similar diminution of the number of Southern oligarchs, notwithstanding the existing numerical disproportion between them and the non-slaveholding whites, whose political freedom, to a rational appreciation, is rather nominal than real. The disease is the same-its workings alone are different. The sword was the soul of Spartan institutions: the pure and elevated conception of the American social structure rests not on physical but on intellectual and moral force; but its deterioration is visible in the new conception of slavery inaugurated and sustained by the militant oligarchs. The process of moral and intellectual decomposition in the South would be still more rapid but for the various influences from the Free States, which, like refreshing breezes, fan its fainting energies.

The sword, it is true, may have decimated whole Spartan communities; but such losses were supplied from the class of the Periokes and other freemen, and even sometimes from the Helots. Domestic slavery devoured the small estates, degraded the freemen, and dried up the sources of political renovation. Five thousand Spartans fought at Plateæ, which gives a total population of about forty thousand. The number of Helots owned by them at that time amounted to one hundred and seventy-five thousand. Subsequently, after the Peloponnesian and Macedonian wars, these Helots were transformed into chattels, and the degenerate Spartans attempted to transform the Periokes into Helots, but made them simply deadly enemies. Almost in proportion as the Spartan oligarchs increased in wealth and possessions, not only did the number of Helots and slaves increase, but military ardor decreased. At Leuctra, Sparta hired her cavalry; and soon after, Sparta, rich in Helots and chattels but poor in citizens, was forced passively to witness the curtailing of her frontiers by Philip of Macedon.

The Helots often revolted; and frequent conspiracies were discovered and subdued in terrible slaughter, when the oligarchs believed themselves again safe. The old laws of most of the American colonies, north and south, contain repeated regulations, dating from the seventeenth and eighteenth centuries, concerning conspiracies, revolts, and tumults perpetrated by negroes; and this, too, several generations before the birth of active abolitionism. For not to abolitionism but to the love of liberty inborn in human nature-in the Spartan Helot as in the colored chattel of the Southern oligarch-are to be attributed the conspiracies continually fermenting among Southern slaves. At times the Spartans were obliged to ask succor from the Athenians and other allies against their revolted Helots. To-day the Union is fully able to suppress servile revolts, but in some future time the South may vainly look in all quarters of the horizon for active allies. It may find some well-wishers among its interested northern sympathizers, but the chattels will have the sympathy of the civilized Christian and heathen world, besides finding allies among the free colored populations of the Antilles. Under England's fatherly and humane direction, these colored populations are being initiated into genuine Christian civilization, and make comparatively great strides and progress in material and political culture, in orderly life, in self-government, in the employment of the free press, and in debating their interests in legislative assemblies and cabinet councils. Ever since the establishment of American slavery on a social and religious basis, the mass of the white population in the South, and, above all, the great heroes, apostles, and combatants of the new political creed, are returning to barbarism-willingly and deliberately renouncing all genuine mental and moral culture. And thus the two extremes may meet in some future emergency-the colored inhabitant of the Antilles as a superior civilized being, will face the barbarized white oppressor in the South.

The Spartan Helot increased with a fecundity fearful for the oligarchs, who resorted to the horrible *kryptea*, or slaughter of unarmed Helots all over Laconia at a time appointed specially and secretly by the ephors. This was the last resort to avert the danger, and more than once was it used during the brilliant epoch of Sparta.

In the South the chattels likewise increase very rapidly, but not rapidly enough to satisfy the breeders, planters, and slave-traders. All things considered, the colored enslaved population increases in a proportion by far more rapid than the white. After 1783 the blacks were estimated at between five and six hundred thousand: the census of 1860 will find them full four millions: and no wonder. Trafficking slave-breeders, as well as planters, organize breeding as systematically as cattle-raisers attend to their stock. In Virginia this is the principal pursuit, and the chief source of income from domestic husbandry. The breeders have small enclosures to gently exercise the young human stock like the breeders of valuable horses. In some States, principally in the cotton region, the colored chattels outnumber the whites; in others the respective numbers are nearly equal. About one hundred and fifty years ago, South Carolina, through the voice of her law-makers, referring to the increase in chattels, declared it an "afflicting providence of God that the white persons do not proportionably multiply." Nowadays South Carolina finds the affliction a blessing. Though her colored population already outnumbers the white, she is first in assaulting humanity by reopening the slave-trade.

Cotton is a plant indigenous to the old world-to Asia and Africa. Its culture by free labor may soon become very profitable in other regions of the globe. Sooner or later this will end the exclusive American monopoly of its production, and then the dead weight of chattelhood will press fearfully on the oligarchs in economical as in social ways, even if the chattels remain quiet: this is, however, impossible to suppose, on account of their continually increasing numbers. Already slaves are tortured, murdered, burnt and slaughtered at the first danger, even though it be imaginary. Now this is done individually, and, even according to Southern notions, illegally. When the profits from slave-labor shall dwindle, and the danger from great masses of chattels shall increase, self-preservation and fatality will force the slaveocracy into attempting to re-enact the Spartan *krypteia*: the cattle-breeder easily transforming himself into the butcher. Even now many of them are on the way to bringing this about, by exposing their old and unproductive field hands to perish from want and misery.

In the course of about four centuries, both during and after the Peloponnesian war, the Spartan oligarchy was enriched more and more by the spoils of victorious wars, and by the importation of slaves as war prisoners from other Greek and from barbarous nations. Then the difference between the rich and poor was more striking, and the eternal process of oppressing the poor, seizing upon their property, or buying them out, was busily and cheerfully pursued. Then Laconia was held by comparatively few Spartan slaveholders-but there were no more heroes of Thermopylæ. Citizens and freemen were a scarcity during the Augustan period; but slaves, the property of a few wealthy owners, actually covered Lacedemonia and Sparta. Domestic slavery undermined and destroyed the Spartan nation in precisely the same manner as it did others before and since. The enslaved Helots and Greeks, and many of the descendants of the enslavers, became, in their turn, slaves of the Romans, then of the Slavic invaders, afterward of the Crusaders, till finally all of them, masters and slaves, groaned under the yoke of the Osmanlis. The traveller can now scarcely find the few mouldering ruins of the once proud and enslaving city. Spartan history covers nearly a thousand years: and for centuries the destructive disease was at work. Some of its symptoms, in the course of half a century, are already highly developed in the South.

Piracy and kidnapping, which in Greece originated at a time when every man saw an enemy almost in his immediate neighbor, did not wholly cease when national relations became more normal and regular. When slavery began to permeate the domestic economy, piracy and the slave-traffic were of course more active. The Southern enslavers assert that their region is not yet supplied with the necessary number of chattels. They draw on piracy, kidnapping, and bloodshed in Africa. The almost incessant wars between the Greek neighboring tribes and nations encouraged slavery; and innocent citizens, going from one Greek state to another, were often enslaved through enmity and greed. However, this savage custom became softened and finally abandoned when the mutual relations became more civilized and regulated; whereas freemen from free states of the Union are arrested and imprisoned in the so-called civilized slave-holding states, and in some cases they can be legally sold as slaves.

In Bœotia slaves were not numerous-being only occasionally made and used. Neither serfs, bond-men, nor chattels, were held in Elis, Locris, or by the Arcadians, Phocians, or Achæans, until the downfall of Greek dignity, liberty, and independence, under the Macedonian and Roman rule. The Phocians prohibited slavery by express legislation.

The Ionians in Attica boasted that they sprang from their native soil. They were therefore the primitive tillers and cultivators of their not over-fertile and rather rocky land, of about one hundred and ninety square miles. This land was divided more or less equally into small homesteads worked by yeomen, to whom chattels would have been a burden. Centuries after the heroic or legendary epoch, when Attica possessed wealthier landowners, Hesiod advises the agriculturists to work their lands by the free labor of the Thetes in preference to slave labor.

Athens became very early a commercial city, and perhaps piratical expeditions for the kidnapping of slaves were fitted out from the Piræus. At any rate, slavery, chattelhood, was especially, if not exclusively, fostered when commerce became more extensive. Athens was the seat and focus of domestic slavery. In the course of time almost all trades were carried on by slaves, as also mining, and finally, farming. But all this was the growth of the long process of centuries.

Debtors were enslaved; but Solon abolished this right of the creditor. He likewise abolished the custom of going about armed in the community. Generally it is a sign of a dangerous and very degraded state of society when men carry arms as a necessity. By a strange coincidence, since slavery has been proclaimed a moral and religious duty, the use of bowie-knives, revolvers, and rifles becomes more and more the order of the day in the South. Not against the slave, not against any foreign enemy, not even against the abolitionist, do the men of the South arm themselves, but it is against each other that they have recourse to armed assaults in their private and public intercourse. From the South the savage custom invades the North, and it has in some cases been forced on peaceful Northern members of Congress in self-defence against the assaults of their Southern colleagues.

The Ionic race had no serfs or Helots, either in Attica or elsewhere. But in Attica, as in other Greek communities, and indeed throughout the whole world, from among the primitive yeomen or peasants, emerged those who, more thrifty, more successful, or more brave, accumulated wealth in various ways. Such was one mode in which aristocracy originated. These yeomen growing richer, acquired more land, bought out smaller farmers, and could hire more field hands. Even before Solon the aim of the rich was to transform freeholders into tenants, but Solon stemmed this current for a long period of time.

Parents could sell their children into slavery; Solon reduced this right to such daughters as willingly submitted to seduction. A poor man could sell himself into slavery, and children exposed by their parents were enslaved by the public authorities.

War and traffic furnished the great supplies of slaves or chattels for the Athenians. Such chattels were from all nations and races, and the black slaves constituted an accidental and imperceptible minority. Witness Æsop telling the story of a rustic who bought a black slave and unsuccessfully tried to bleach or to whitewash it. If blacks had been common merchandise, the rustic would have been familiar with its nature. Slavery was transmitted from parents to children, if the prisoner of war was not ransomed or the slave not manumitted. But at any time a slave could receive or buy his freedom, and a chattel once liberated could not, under penalty of capital punishment, again be violently enslaved. In the South they begin to legislate for the re-enslavement of the liberated: the odium no longer falls on the individual but on the whole body politic. All over the ancient world the state watched over and protected the once enfranchised slave: the modern slave-holding polity expels him or legislates for his disfranchisement. In Athens, as all over Greece, the offspring of freemen and slave-women were free.

At first slaves performed domestic service, and afterward, when their number increased, they were employed in various trades. The state used them in public works, sometimes to row the ships. But the greatest number were employed to work the mills and mines of Attica. However, the state itself did not work the mines, but rented them generally without the slave labor; though private individuals rented them for a term of years, together with the slaves who worked them. Slowly chattelhood spread over the rural economy of Attica.

About the time of the Persian wars, rural property was still nearly equally divided among the citizens. Wealth was accumulated and represented in commerce, in various industries, and in the precious metals. But at that time slaves nowhere outnumbered the freemen. At the battle of Marathon the Athenians had ten thousand *hoplites* or heavily armed able-bodied citizens; at Platea eight thousand; and in both battles nearly as many *peltasts* or lightly-armed troops-poorer citizens, but not serfs, or retainers, or slaves. Before the invasion of Xerxes, the free population of Attica probably amounted to more than one hundred and twenty thousand of both sexes and all ages. The slave population is estimated at the utmost as sixty thousand.

Athens, like all the other Greek republics, colonized other countries with the surplus of their free-mostly poor-population. Herodotus died in such an expedition. The Dorians very likely colonized Sicily, the Ionians Italy or Magna Grecia. Such colonizations relieved the over-populated mother-country, extended the Hellenic culture, but likewise, in more than one way, fostered and nursed slavery. The Greek colonists in Sicily and in Italy, conquering or pushing into the interior the aborigines of these lands, enslaved, kidnapped and sold them. Then the Greek cities warred with and enslaved each other. Such was the case between Sybaris and Crotona, or in Sicily between Syracuse, Girgentum, etc. The rich men of Athens bought more and more slaves, purchased the lands of the poor, substituted in various handicrafts their gangs of slave laborers for freemen, and exported the impoverished freemen.[13] The increase of large estates and chattels went hand in hand with the decrease of freemen and public spirit in Athens; and the same was the case in other large commercial cities of Greece.

After the Persian war Athens became the wealthiest of commercial cities, and the Athenians a conquering nation. Both circumstances increased the number of slaves. But still the landed property was not yet absorbed. Alcibiades owned only about three hundred *plethra*, or about seventy-five acres of land in Attica. The wealthy slave-owners and oligarchs were not in power, but they owned mines in Attica and landed estates in various Greek dependencies and colonies. Slavery prevailed in the city, and it became more and more common on the farms. However, on the eve of the Peloponnesian war, democracy still prevailed. The oligarchs, proud of their slaves, mines, plantations and estates, scorned the democracy of Athens, composed of artists, yeomen, operatives, artisans-who really formed the soul of the great Periclean epoch.

Oligarchies are alike all over the world; in most of them, slave-holders, however called, live upon the labor of others; all of them scorn the laboring classes. The Southern militant planters and their Northern servile retainers scorn the enlightened masses of working-men, the farmers and operatives of the free states. But it is those masses which exclusively give original signification to America in the history of human development. Athens and the various monuments of the Periclean epoch coruscate over doomed Hellas: so the villages of the free states, with their schools and laborious, intelligent, self-reliant populations, shed their rays now over the Christian world. And the sight of such a village is a far different subject of contemplation from that of the slave-crowded plantation.

Slavery increased rapidly in Athens, as in all the great commercial centres, and in the adjacent isles of Greece. At the beginning of the Peloponnesian war, Attica had a population of about twenty thousand male adults, or a little over one hundred thousand free persons of all ages and sexes. The whole free population of Greece is estimated to have been at that time about eight hundred thousand souls; and the slaves-the Spartan serfs or Helots included-perhaps outnumbered the freemen. Thucydides says that the island of Chios had about two hundred and ten thousand slaves, the largest number next to Sparta; then came Athens, with nearly two hundred thousand human chattels; while other great commercial cities of Greece, as Sycyon and Corinth, likewise contained very large numbers.

The Peloponnesian war was waged with all the violence of a family feud. It spread desolation, impoverishment, carnage and slavery over Greece. Captives made by the one or the other contending party, were sold by tens of thousands into slavery; these captives were principally the small freeholders, the *thetes* and *geomori* —operatives, artisans, and, indeed, free workmen of every kind. Their number consequently diminished, and their small estates were either bought or taken violently by the rich, who thus simultaneously increased the number of their chattels and their acres of land. Thus did slavery permeate more and more the Greek social polity, until, at the epoch between Pericles and the beginning of the Macedonian wars, the number of slaves in Athens and Attica was nearly doubled: but the free population did not thus increase. Large landed estates became more and more common, till, in the time of Demosthenes, the soil of Attica, was concentrated in comparatively few hands. At Cheronea, the Athenians fought against Philip with mercenary troops, and even armed their slaves. But the spirit of Marathon and of Platæa was gone, and Athens succumbed. The gold of Philip was acceptable to the rich slave-holders, and went principally into the hands of the oligarchs; but alas! no second Miltiades ever emerged from their ranks.

It is supposed that at the epoch of the Macedonian conquest, the proportion of slaves and freemen was as seven to three. Near the beginning of the reign of Alexander, the free population of Greece amounted to one million, and the slaves to one million four hundred and thirty-five thousand. The census taken in Attica about that time, under the archon Demetrius of Phaleris, gives for Athens and Attica twenty-one thousand adult male citizens, or a little over one hundred thousand persons of all ages and sexes, and four hundred thousand slaves. The slave population pre-ponderated, however, only in the wealthy part of Greece; the poorer agricultural communities, as already mentioned, having been free from its curse. Thus Corinth had four hundred and fifty thousand, and Ægina four hundred and seventy thousand slaves; and this is the reason that Philip, Alexander, Antipater, and other conquerors had such comparatively easy work in destroying Greek liberty.

The Macedonian wars also spread desolation, slavery and ruin; and of Thebans alone, Alexander sold over thirty thousand into slavery.

Thus ended the independent political existence of Greece and Athens. Rich slave-holders, indeed, they still had; but they ceased to have a history of their own, or a distinct political existence; and Greece became a satellite successively of Macedonia, Syria, Egypt and Rome.

To conclude: in Athens, as indeed throughout Greece, the commercial cities inaugurated domestic slavery. Slavery first penetrated into domestic life; then entered into the various trades and industries, and finally, almost wholly absorbed the lands and the agricultural economy. It also penetrated into the functions of state, and various minor offices were held by slaves-which anomaly was afterward reproduced in Rome, especially under the emperors.

In the slave section of our own country the system has already got possession of domestic and family life, of agriculture, and of some of the handicrafts; and slaves are employed on some of the railroads as brake-men and assistant-engineers. This may be a cheering proof of the intellectual capacity of the colored race, but it proves also the analogy which exists everywhere between the workings of slavery, whatever may be the distance of ages or the color of the enslaved.

It was only during the period of the moral, social and political decomposition of Greece that slavery flourished. A certain Diophantus at one period proposed a law to enslave all the laborers, artisans and operatives in Athens-so that those who now so loudly demand the same thing here, had prototypes more than twenty-four centuries ago; for, though history has transmitted to infamous memory only the name of Diophantus, yet undoubtedly he stood not alone.

In Athens and in Greece we see the cancer growing steadily over the whole social and political organism, until all Attica and almost the whole of the ancient world were divided only between slave-holders and chattels.

In the slave marts of Athens and of Corinth, and afterward in that of Delos, the sale of chattels was conducted in precisely the same way as it now is in Richmond, in New Orleans and in Memphis. The proceedings of the auctioneers and the traders, of the buyers and the sellers, were as cruel then as they are now. The same eulogies of the capacities of able-bodied men, the same piquant descriptions of the various attractions of the women, the same tricks to conceal bodily defects, and similar guaranties between vender and buyer, then as now.

When, finally, laborers of almost every kind, handicraftsmen and agriculturists, had thus become enslaved, all the freemen, both rich and poor, were speedily swallowed up in an equal degradation. The family became disorganized; the republics perished. This was completely accomplished when Greece passed from Macedonian to Roman rule: then domestic slavery flourished as never before. In that final struggle the password of the Greek slave-holders was, "*Unless we are quickly lost, we cannot be saved.*" The non-slaveholding mountaineers of Achaia fought against the Romans until they were almost exterminated. But Rome conquered, and large numbers of Greeks were sold into slavery by the Roman consuls. Paulus Emilius alone sold one hundred and fifty thousand Macedonians and other Greeks, while the whole population of Corinth was sold by Mummius; and Sylla depopulated Athens, the Piræus and Thebes. The Roman rule in Greece and over the Greek world was a fierce stimulant to the growth of domestic slavery. The Roman senate and the Roman proconsuls especially favored the large slaveholders, since they were the fittest persons to tolerate the yoke. The Romans helped them to degrade and to enslave as much as possible. Rome wanted not freemen in Greece, but slaves and obedient slave-drivers; and Roman tax-gatherers and the farmers of public revenues sold freemen into slavery for debt. Finally, the celebrated Cilician pirates desolated Greece, carrying away and selling, in Delos, almost the last remnants of the free laboring population.

A small body of free citizens now ruled immense masses of slaves. The normal economy of nature was thus destroyed, and the depopulation of Greece went on rapidly. At the time of Cicero, almost the whole of Attica formed the estate of a single slaveholder, who also owned other estates in other parts of Greece. Many militant slave oligarchs doubtless envy that Athenian slaveholder; at any rate they are doing their utmost to bring the Southern States to a condition similar to that just depicted in Athens and Greece.

During the Peloponnesian wars, insurrections of slaves often took place in Attica, especially in the mines. But the greatest slave rebellion, as far as history has recorded, was under the Roman administration. The revolted slaves then seized upon the fortress of Sunium, and for a long time fought bravely for their freedom.

The Greeks, as in some degree all the peoples of antiquity, considered domestic slavery a social misfortune to the enslavers, and an accursed fatality inherent in human society. They never presented it under the false colors of a normal and integral social element. The striking analogies between the workings of slavery in the ancient world and in the American republic, show that the disease is everywhere and eternally the same, and that it does not *ennoble* either the community or the individual slaveholder, as the pro-slavery combatants apodictically assert.

If in the despotic oriental empires, domestic and political slavery at times played into each other's hands until they jointly destroyed national life, *it was domestic slavery, single-handed, which did the work in Greece*, and particularly in Sparta and Athens. Domestic slavery enervated the nation and made it an easy prey to foreign conquest. It converted into a putrescent mass the once great and brilliant Grecian world.

XII. Romans-The Republicans

AUTHORITIES:

Corpus Juris, Livy, Dionysius of Halicarnassus, Niebuhr, Arnold, Savigny, Puchta, Mommsen, Jhring, Clinton, Carl Hegel, Zumpt, etc.

The primitive occupants of the Mediterranean peninsula-anciently, and at the present time, called Italy-issued from the same Aryan stock as peopled Greece. These immigrants, almost from the first moment of their arrival, seem to have devoted themselves to agriculture, as all the relics still dimly visible in prehistoric twilight certify to this fact. Thus, the domestic legend of the Samnites makes an ox the leader of the primitive colonies, which is only a different version of another tradition, according to which Vitulus or Italus —a legendary king, from whom the name of "Italy" is derived-brought about among his subjects the transition from shepherds to farmers. The name *Italia*, in ancient Latin, signified a *country full of cattle*. The oldest of the Latin tribes has the name of *Siculi*, *Sicani*, reapers, and another, *Opsci*, or field-laborers. Among the Italians (or *Italos*, *Italiots*), the legends, creeds, laws, and manners all originate in agriculture; while every one knows the use of the plough in the distant background of the legendary foundation of Rome. The oldest Roman matrimonial rite, the *confarreatio*, also has its name from *rye*. With agriculture is primarily connected a fixed abode, and thus springs up the love of home and family. From agricultural life arises the tribe or clan, which is simply a community of individuals descending from the same ancestor. In this primitive condition the field-labors and domestic occupations were performed by various members, first of the family, and then of the clan. The *servus* or servant of that epoch was no more a chattel in the Latin agricultural family and community than was the primitive servant in the tent of the patriarchs (see "Hebrews" and "Aryas"), or than were the servants of the first colonists in New England, Virginia, or the Carolinas. In these primitive households there were no duties for a chattel, for from the earliest time agricultural and household occupations were as sacred to the yeomen and peasants of Latium and Rome as were the domestic hearth, the father, and the family.

From the left bank of the Tiber to the Volscian mountains, and over the plains of the Campagna, lived the Latins-the *prisci Latini*. They were divided into numerous distinct families or clans, which afterward were the generators of the Roman people. The region where they first appear, in the most ancient times, was therefore settled by separate families, and divided into separate townships and villages. These clans it was which afterward in "the city" constituted the primitive *tribus rusticæ* or rural tribes.

The *Ramnes*, *Ramneis*, *Romaneis*, *Romani* or Romans, the founders of Rome, were, in all probability, bold rovers and adventurers from the various tribes and villages of Latium. They lived among the bushes and groves of the Palatine Mount, and what they acquired by depredation was common property. These primitive legendary Romans had no use for slaves; they had no mart in which to sell them, and it is probable that they neither kidnapped nor enslaved any of the neighboring villagers. Neither legend nor history fixes positively how long these *Ramnenses* or Romans persevered in their wild mode of life. The legend very soon unites them with other settled families, such as the Sabine farmers and peasantry. Then began the specific organized existence of the Romans.

The whole soil of the Roman community constituted an *ager Romanus* or *publicus*. Every citizen, as a part of the *populus* or state, received therefrom a share of the public land for his private use. When the Romans extended their dominions by subduing the neighboring villages and districts, the lands of such districts, their pasturages, etc., were incorporated into the *ager Romanus*, and the inhabitants were sometimes obliged to settle in Rome or in lands in its vicinity. From these originated the plebeians, who, under certain conditions, received shares or lots in the *ager publicus* or *Romanus*. The aim of these primitive wars was neither to kidnap nor enslave the subdued tribes, nor even to transform them into serfs or Helots, at the utmost to make them tributaries.

To the legendary Romulus were attributed the regulations or laws which forbade the massacre or enslavement of the male youth of conquered villages or districts, and prohibited also the transformation of the conquered lands into pasturages, and provided that they should be parcelled into small homesteads for Roman citizens. At first two acres, and afterward seven, constituted such a civic patrimony or homestead. It was the abandonment of this law in after ages which generated slavery and the ruin of the populace.

Only the prisoners made on the battle-field and counted among the spoils, were sold by the state at public auction: *sub hasta*, "under the spear," and *sub corona*, "the citizen wearing a crown" —to the citizens or members of the community. Such prisoner, like all other vended booty, became a *mancipium, res mancipia,* (from *manu capere,* "taken, caught by the hand.") Such slaves, in all probability, were not numerous. A more prolific source of slavery was the right to enslave a debtor for life. The debtor became a *mancipium*; and even when the right to enslave him was abolished, the legal formality of catching him or touching by the hand, was maintained.

The power of the father or chief of the household —*patria potestas* —was limitless, in the precincts of the house, over both the family and the servants. The father, be he patrician or plebeian, could sell his son into slavery, but the right was very seldom used. So also, the father had the right of life and death over all his family and household. Manumission of slaves was common; it existed from the most ancient times. The slave could also buy his liberty. Subsequently, in the last centuries of the republic and under the emperors, a slave could be emancipated by various positive enactments, and the status of the manumitted slave often passed through various gradations before reaching absolute independence. The fortieth book of the Pandects contains several chapters relating to manumission.

Sometimes, though rarely, under the kings, the *public slaves* —or those of the state, exclusively war prisoners-were employed on public works, or to take care of public buildings, or to attend on magistrates or priests. The condition of public slaves was preferable to that of the private slaves; indeed, the former subsequently had the right to dispose by will of half of their property.

The land was tilled by the hands of the senators themselves, patricians though they were. If a patrician (*pater*) possessed more land than he could cultivate himself, he divided it among small free cultivators, or let it out; and no servile hand desecrated the plough. The slaves employed in the house were not numerous.

King Servius Tullius inaugurated a political reform, intended to alleviate the condition of the plebeians oppressed by the patricians; and in preparation for it he took a census. At that time Rome had eighty-four thousand able-bodied citizens between the ages of eighteen and sixty years, or a total population of about four hundred thousand free persons of all ages and sexes. To this number must be added the plebeians, who were not yet citizens. The artisans, operatives, clients and strangers perhaps doubled this estimate of the population of Rome, the limits of which then stretched from the Tiber to the Anio, including, probably, the lands of Alba, and making in all, an area of about one hundred and twenty or one hundred and forty square miles. There would thus be more than five thousand five hundred inhabitants to a square mile; so that there could have remained but very little room for slaves.

In the first stages of the republic, the patricians continually increased their landed estates, and by renting these to tenants, they acquired power over the poor free laborers, and by lending them money, got a claim on their bodies and also on the free yeomen and rustics. The patricians were hard creditors, and rigorously availed themselves of their legal rights, and their *ergastula* —caves or vaulted prisons-were almost continually filled with poor debtors. This impoverishment of the free yeomanry increased after the terrible devastations perpetrated by the Gauls under Brennus. Finally, these financial oppressions generated those revolts of the plebeians which terminated in their obtaining political rights and full citizenship, together with the jurisprudential reform known as the Twelve Tables.

During the first three or four centuries of the republic, the number of slaves who were non-debtors was very limited. At the census made in the year of Rome 280, the free population amounted to over four hundred and ten thousand persons, and there were then only seventeen thousand slaves.

Few, if any, women were originally enslaved. If the nursling of a Roman family often drew its milk from the paps of a slave woman, the Roman matron, in turn, often gave her breast to the babe of a slave.

In those early times the slaves were kindly treated; they were regarded rather as members of the family than as chattels; they took their meals with their masters, and participated in the sacrifices and worship of the gods. They were not considered dangerous elements in the household or the state. From that early epoch also date certain privileges conceded to the slaves-such as their earnings or *peculium*, which, at first established only by common usage, became afterward defined and specified by the civil law, in which originally the slave was almost entirely ignored.

Plebeians, proletarians, clients, free artisans-almost all of whom were Romans-formed, in the first centuries, the bulk of the slaves kept in the *ergastula* of the patricians. Frequently, when a consul wanted soldiers, he would order the creditors to open their vaults and disgorge the victims for his service in a campaign. And sometimes, though rarely, a consular edict quashed the debts and set them free.

In these earliest times of the Republic the name of a *proletarius*, or procreator of children, was held in honor. It was to an increase of the number of its freemen, not of its slaves, that the Republic hoped for duration and power. To be called *colonus*, or a cultivator, was also an honor to a Roman citizen, whether patrician or plebeian, in the times of Cincinnatus, Dentatus, and Regulus. Labor was then a high distinction, nay it was sacred; and a slave may almost be considered an accident in domestic pursuits. Scaurus, then one of the wealthiest and most powerful senators, had six slaves, Curius Dentatus one, Regulus one, when he commanded the Roman legions against Carthage, while Cincinnatus may have had one, but most probably none.

The three hundred patrician Fabii, who left Rome, crossed the Tiber and settled at the utmost limits of the state, to guard and defend it from the inroads of invaders-were yeomen, ploughmen, and farmers. And without intending to offend or disparage the *ennobled* pro-slavery militants of this age and country, one may surely suppose that they have at least a little respect for the names and the character of a Dentatus, a Cincinnatus, and a Regulus.

However, the patricians and many of the rich plebeians continued uninterruptedly to increase their lands in the *ager publicus* at the cost of the smaller yeomen, and that at a time when rural slavery may be said to have been in its infancy. And it was the object of the celebrated agrarian laws to restore the balance between the rich and the poor in the possession of the public lands.

The wars carried on by Rome with the Greek cities in Italy, which were crowded with slaves, and the wars carried on beyond the borders of Italy, were the great nurseries of slavery. In such wars free citizens were of course killed in vast numbers, and slave war-prisoners were brought back to Rome in their stead. The Punic wars are the turning point in the political history and in the social and moral development of the Romans. These wars gave the first great stimulus both to urbane, and rustic slavery. Urbane slaves were those employed in houses and villas for personal service; rustic slaves were those engaged in working the estates.

Rome became more and more a maritime and commercial emporium, and slaves were now imported as merchandise, besides the continually increasing number of prisoners of war. Thus Regulus brought over twenty thousand Carthaginians of all conditions of life, who were sold into slavery. But even at the time of the second Punic war, the number of slaves of all kinds must have been comparatively very small; for after the terrible defeat at Cannæ, the Roman senate ordered the slaves to be armed, and only eight thousand were inscribed on the military roll. The census taken about that time gave, in all the state, two hundred and thirty-seven thousand Roman adult citizens, or 1,185,000 free persons of all sexes and ages; making in all, 770,000 Romans, with their Italian allies, fit for military duty.

The victorious Hannibal sold into slavery thousands of Roman citizens; while the final conquest of the Carthaginian empire and of Sicily poured many thousands of slaves into Rome from Africa, from Sicily, and from Spain. Thus thirty thousand inhabitants of Palermo and twenty-five thousand of Agrigentum, were sold into slavery. Among those brought by Scipio from Africa, were two thousand artisans whom he promised he would not sell, but would keep as slaves of the state.

Henceforth conquests in and out of Italy became a social and political necessity for Rome. The spoils and lands rapidly increased the wealth of the citizens, but principally of the patricians. The habits of luxury, the contempt of manual and especially agricultural labor, became general; and with it the demand increased for slaves to work the estates and to cater to the other wants of the rich and effeminate Romans. So now again, war and rapine, the annexation of Mexico, Central America, Cuba and Hayti, are the aims of the militant American slaveocracy.

In course of time Rome became a mart for slaves, as great as were Carthage, Corinth, Athens and Syracuse. The slave market, like all the other markets in the city, was superintended by the ædiles. The municipal regulations compelled the vender to hang a scroll around the neck of the slave, containing a description of his character, in which his defects were declared and his health warranted, especially his freedom from epilepsy and violent diseases. The nativity of the slave was considered important and was also to be declared. When the Romans conquered Asia, the Syrians (who belonged to the Caucasian race) were considered to be especially adapted for slavery, just as the negroes are at the present day. An incalculable majority of the Roman slaves were of the Caucasian or Japhetic race. Where, oh, where, during these almost countless centuries, slept the Scriptural curse of Ham?

The Hannibalian war was eminently destructive to the yeomanry and to their small homesteads. Internal domestic economy was shaken from the foundation and almost entirely destroyed; the arable lands were rapidly turned into wild sheep pastures, with wild slaves on them as shepherds; the patricians no longer considered agriculture their first occupation, when they found that the slaves of Sicily, Africa, and afterward Egypt, were able to nourish both them and the people; and any land still in culture, was worked by poor farmers, by colonists and slaves. The term *colonist*, also, now acquired a somewhat degraded signification, for they were now but poor proletarians and plebeians. Now also came into more common use the legal denomination *familia rustica*, or rural chattels; and perhaps at this time, or soon after, originated in Rome the proverb: *"As many slaves, so many enemies."*

In the course of the sixth century, U.C., there burst out in great force the antagonism between the free rural laborer and the slave. The struggle for life and death between the large land and slave holders and the yeomanry or freeholders, became more and more active. That which had taken root but slowly in the previous centuries, became strengthened by contact with nations of older and more corrupt civilizations. The influence of Carthage appeared in the rural economy of the Romans, and they began to model their agriculture on the Carthaginian slave husbandry. The book on "Agriculture," written by Magon, a Carthaginian, was translated into Latin by order of the senate. The country was rapidly filled with slaves, and now originated that reckless cruelty in dealing with them which was reflected soon after in the laws. The large slaveholders continually enlarged their estates by buying or seizing under various pretexts the small homesteads. In the times of Publicola and of the Twelve Tables, the small freeholders had been driven to despair by debts and executions; but now they were ruined and utterly destroyed by slave labor. The patricians, who had formerly been mortgagees of homesteads, and for whom the freeholder had worked to quash his indebtedness, now became large planters. Thus in Rome and throughout Italy, as well as in the conquered provinces, the slave tide rose higher and higher. These provinces constituted the estates of the sovereign Roman people; but in their administration the patricians applied the same discipline, the same iron rod that they held over their slaves. They kept the ironed chattels in walled courts and prisons, and it became proverbial that "A good mastiff should show no mercy to slaves"—a proverb still applicable to the bloodhounds of slavery.

The poor freemen, expelled from the country and deprived of employment, crowded more and more into Rome, increasing, to a fearful extent, the Roman proletariate. For more than three centuries the best men of Rome, Crassus, Licinius, Emilianus, Drusus, and the Gracchi, made various efforts, to arrest by agrarian laws, the destruction of freeholds, first by the large estates, and then by slaveholders. These efforts were the principal causes of the internal struggles and civil wars of the Roman republic, and their failure proved the destruction of the Roman world. Scipio Æmilianus Africanus prophecied the downfall of liberty and of the Roman state, if this substitution of plantation economy for the old yeomanry and freeholds did not cease. About the year 620 U.C., scarcely any freeholds for yeomen existed in Etruria; and Plutarch says, "When Tiberius Gracchus went through Tuscany to Numantia he found the country almost depopulated, there being scarcely any free husbandmen or free shepherds, but for the most part imported slaves. He then first conceived the course of policy," etc. An account almost precisely similar of the present condition of Virginia may be found in a speech made a few years ago by one of her own sons-one, too, of the most ardent upholders of slavery, whether as governor of the state, as active politician, or as a private citizen. The Roman planter desolated Etruria by devoting it to the breeding of cattle; the Virginian desolates her prolific soil and his own manhood by devoting them to the breeding of "niggers." But here the analogy ceases. The Virginian savior will stand in history the antipodes of the Gracchi.

The Roman oligarchs, slaveholders and slave-traders, baffled the sublime efforts of the Gracchi, who attempted not only to preserve but to increase the number of freeholders. The Gracchi were murdered by the oligarchs and the degraded rabble. Publius Scipio Nasica and other senators, fomented and incited Publius Satureius and Lucius Rufus, who, armed with bludgeons or legs of broken chairs, struck down and murdered Tiberius Gracchus. With similar barbarity Senator Sumner was assaulted in his chair of office; and Senators Toombs and Mason, as well as Hons. Keitt and Brooks, had thus their bloody prototypes in Rome. The murder of the Gracchi was applauded by the degraded Roman rabble; so also did the "poor whites" in the South applaud the assault on Sumner, as well as every other act of savage violence perpetrated in Washington or elsewhere in the interests of slavery. The Roman men and matrons, however, did not present *cudgels of honor* to Publius Satureius and Lucius Rufus.

The current of slavery now flowed in unchecked course, ever enlarging as it advanced. The free citizens, deprived of their homes and property, though now inspired no more by the antique Roman virtue, nevertheless preserved somewhat of their former bravery, and the legions extended the Roman sway over Greece and Asia. The captives taken from the cities and districts were no longer colonized, as formerly, but were sold into slavery like prisoners made on the battle-field, and the most vigorous and patriotic portion of the population of other countries was sold as chattels. The depopulation of Macedon, Epirus, and Greece by the Roman conquerors, has been already mentioned. Cato brought large numbers of slaves from Cyprus; Lucullus must have made innumerable thousands in Bithynia and Cappadocia, judging from the low price of about two-thirds of a dollar per head, for which his human booty was sold. Marius made slaves of more than one hundred and fifty thousand Gauls, Kymri and Teutons, and among them undoubtedly many Angles and Saxons.

The exactions, taxes and tributes which the Roman oligarchy compelled the conquered kingdoms to pay, increased the general poverty, ruin and slavery. The men and children of the Sicilians and other nations were sold into slavery by the Roman tax gatherers: and when Marius demanded from Nicomede of Bithynia, as an ally, his contingent of troops, the king made answer that all his able-bodied men were sold into slavery by the Roman tax and tribute gatherers. And even to the present day, in the slave states, they sell into slavery free men and women for the costs of prison and judgment.

All these slaves, either in person or cash, centred toward Rome, and thus increased the power and resources of the oligarch slaveholders, while at the same time they incontinently devoured the domestic economy of the state; and the impoverished and homeless freemen took their revenge on the oligarchs under Marius, father and son, and under Cinna; while Sylla, in turn, was the avenging sword of the oligarchs and slaveholders. In his time slaveholders were composed principally of wealthy ancient patricians and new rich men or cavaliers, who together constituted the oligarchy of capital: just as now, the "old families," as they are called, of the slave states combine with the new plantation-buyers, overseers, traders, etc., and jointly form the slave-driving oligarchy.

Sylla shed in torrents the blood of those who dared to hope for a reform from Marius and the reduction of the power of the slaveholders. He was their soul and their representative, and was guilty of every cruelty to uphold the interest, not of Rome, but of the egotistical oligarchy; just, again, as in the slave states, the diminutive would-be Syllas are ready to sacrifice every thing to maintain slavery, even to the destruction of society and the republic; while the public spirit of a free state makes every freeman seek his own welfare in the general good.

In the time of Sylla, Italy contained about thirteen millions of slaves; and slave insurrections, both there and in Sicily, succeeded each other almost uninterruptedly. History has recorded some of them, and immortalized the name of the heroic Spartacus. The insurrection in Sicily also, under Ennus, lasted more than four years, and cost the lives of nearly a million of victims.

Slave-breeding was not yet conducted on a large scale. The advice of Cato the Grumbler, was against its permission; and he obliged his slaves to pay him a tax from their *peculium* whenever they cohabited with the other sex.

The large amount of grain imported from conquered countries cultivated by slaves, brought about a competition which soon destroyed the homesteads of the yeomanry, and transformed the fertile Campagna and almost the whole of Italy into a vast cattle pasturage.

It has been already mentioned (see "Greeks") that during the post-Alexandrian dissolution of Greece and of the east, Cilician piracy was rampant in the eastern part of the Mediterranean. Until Pompey destroyed this piracy, it had its centres and markets in Crete, in Rhodes, and even in Alexandria; but the principal mart was in Delos, where sometimes ten thousand slaves changed masters in a single day. The Roman merchants were the best patrons of the Cilician pirates; and recent developments show that our slave-planters are again beginning to be willing customers to the Americo-African pirates and slave-traders. In general, wherever the capitalist-slaveholder is permitted to develop his supremacy in a state, both man and society are materially and morally ruined. Thus it was with Rome and Italy at that epoch: and so also, the American slave states move on rapidly in the orbit from which Rome whirled into the abyss.

In the Mithridatic and Asiatic wars, Pompey enslaved more than two millions of Asiatics; and according to the census made under him, Italy contained at that time only 450,000 able-bodied citizens capable of military duty, or a total free population of about 2,200,000. It is also asserted that Cæsar enslaved at least one million of Gauls. In the age of Cicero only about two thousand citizens of Rome possessed landed property, but with it they owned legions of chattels; and Cicero —a parvenu without manhood, first the accessory and then the betrayer of Cataline-maintained that only slaveholders could be considered respectable.

After the patricians were restored to power by Sylla, they found that war and hereditary slavery did not supply the necessary quantity of slaves; and they consequently began to kidnap and enslave poor freemen-even their Roman fellow-citizens. To rob and take violent possession of the remaining freeholds became now a matter of course. In the time of Cicero nearly all handicrafts in the city, which had once been in the hands of freemen and clients, were carried on by slaves, either directly for their masters, or indirectly by being hired out to others. It became more and more common to hire out skilful slaves and to train them up with the view of receiving the revenues of their proficiency. It was then just as it is now; for then Italy, as now the slave states, was owned by slave-drivers, worked by slaves, and guarded by heartless overseers and bloodhounds.

In the beginning of his career, Cæsar tried to create a free yeomanry by distributing the public domain among the poor free citizens and the disabled soldiers. After the victory over the oligarchs and Pompey, he colonized eighty thousand of the proletarians of Rome. But it was forever too late; and besides, the oligarchs and slaveholders opposed his attempts. Scarcely any free laborers existed; the domain of the slave-driver was universal; indeed it was such an epoch as is now again so ardently desired by small senators, would-be statesmen, and the whole vanguard of the knight-errant army of chattelhood. Freeholds disappeared from Italy, and almost from the world, with the exception perhaps of the valleys in the Apennines and the Abruzzi. The region from the modern Civita Vecchia across Tusculum to Boiæ and Naples, where once a dense population of Latin and Italian free yeomanry ploughed the soil and reaped the harvest, was now covered with splendid villas for the masters and with *ergastula* for their chattels. But the proud inhabitants of the villas, the rich patricians and slaveholders, were themselves soon to become political slaves. Central Italy and the lands around Rome which nursed the armies, and from which were recruited the conquerors of the Carthaginians, Numidians and the phalanxes of Macedonia, was now a waste, depopulated solitude, owned by a few wealthy planters.

Domestic slavery now brought Rome into the condition to which it had reduced Greece and the oriental world centuries before. The Italy of Varro and of Cicero resembled the Greece of Polybius, Carthage on the eve of its fall, or Asia as found by Alexander. *What will be the full and ripe crop of this dragon-teeth-seed in America?* Whenever domestic slavery is planted and takes enduring root in a country, even the beauty of nature is ravaged and destroyed. Do the chattel-cabins enliven the landscape of Virginia or beautify the coast of Carolina? The living rill or river gloriously reflects a thousandfold the rays and colors of light, but stagnant sewers are everywhere alike fetid and abominable.

During the epoch when slavery flourished and the Roman republic fell into decay, those terrible cruelties toward slaves which history records, and which even now strike the mind with horror, came into vogue. Slaves, chained in gangs, worked in the fields; at night they were crowded together in prisons; a Greek letter was branded with a hot iron into their cheeks, and other unmentionable cruelties were practised. Still, even then, they were comparatively well fed, as indeed are all useful and submissive beasts. The Roman fabulist Phœdrus, in his tale of "*The Dog and the Wolf*," tells how this good feeding was regarded by the nobler minds of that demoralized epoch.

After the time of Cato the breeding of slaves became more general, and one woman would frequently nurse several babies, while their mothers were otherwise employed. This became even more common, however, in a subsequent epoch.

Slaves were used for all purposes in the household of the rich Roman oligarch. They performed the highest as well as the basest labors; they were even doctors, architects, literati, readers and amanuenses; they exercised in some degree the function of printing in our day, as by their labor manuscripts were copied and libraries formed.

How domestic slavery degraded the Roman slaveholder is evidenced by the direct statements of history, as well as by the descriptions of manners in the comedies, etc., which have reached us from that epoch. In proportion as the old Roman spirit and courage declined, did violence and rowdyism increase. Among the various deleterious influences of slavery on slaveholders, also, two which are very noticeable at that remote time, may again, after the lapse of ages, be observed under our own eyes: slavery either emasculates the slaveholder physically and mentally, and thus renders him cruel from effeminacy; or else makes him rude and reckless, and full of a coarse and savage ferocity.

The Roman oligarchs had all the polish reflected from general culture covering the most depraved minds; and this told upon their politics as well as upon their domestic economy. As early as the time of Jugurtha, nearly all the senators were venal; and subsequently, those who preserved individually some of the better Roman characteristics, became even more rare. Such an one, toward the end of the republic, was Sextus Roscius, whom history mentions for his good treatment of his bondmen. Whenever a special class of society becomes anywhere predominant, a special type of character is formed as the standard of honor, which, however, is generally quite different from the true standard of an honest man or an upright citizen. But, false criterions aside, the Slave States may, and undoubtedly do, possess many honorable planters and citizens, as Carroll of Carrollton or Aiken and Preston of South Carolina: but none of these men give tone or character to the manners or the laws; their influence is not permitted in Congress or the state legislatures, nor are their opinions reflected in the press or in the sham literature and science of their section. But the customs and manners which now prevail, the laws enacted, the utterances of statesmen, the condition of science and literature, and the statements of the current press, constitute the evidence from which the social condition of the nation is to be judged now, and the historic evidence from which it will be judged by future generations.

The slaveholding oligarchy triumphed over Marius and Sertorius as it triumphed over the Gracchi. *And the Roman republic expired* composed of slaveholders, capitalists, and beggars. The fury of the indignant and impoverished people carried Cæsar to power over the carcasses and the ruins of the oligarchy, which long before had reduced the liberty and the name of the Roman people to a sham and a mockery. Domestic slavery for several centuries undermined the Roman republic, and its corrosive action increased with the most brilliant periods of conquest, just as the human body, though gnawed internally by a chronic disease, may exhibit, for a longer or shorter period, all the appearances of health and vigor. Oligarchs, slaveholders, and capitalists destroyed a republic founded by intelligent and industrious agriculturists, yeomen, and freeholders.

More than one point of analogy exists between the Roman and American republics. Independent and intelligent small farmers, with artisans, mechanics, etc., were the founders of American independence. And the free states have not only preserved but elevated to a higher social and political significance the original characteristics of her existence; and the reproaches hurled by the militant pro-slavery oligarchs against the free farmers and operatives in the fields and workshops of the north are sacrilegious to liberty and light. Even so the prince of darkness curses the god of day!

XIII. Romans-Political Slaves

It was an easy matter to engraft despotism upon a society morally, politically, and economically ruined by the slaveholding oligarchy. The Cæsars and the emperors inaugurated and developed it, and at that time nothing else would have suited Rome. Domestic slavery had destroyed the republican spirit, and the vitality of ancient republican institutions. The political condition of the empire-that world-ruling despotism-under the Cæsars and the emperors[14] was the legitimate result of chattelhood and of oligarchism. Political and domestic slavery now went hand in hand, both of them supreme over man and society.

During the reign of the six Cæsars, rural as well as urban slavery rapidly began to be reduced to method and to legal forms. Augustus tried to modify somewhat the cruel treatment of the slaves: he abolished, for instance, the custom of branding their cheeks with a hot iron, and ordered instead that they should wear metallic collars. It came into vogue, also, that a woman who had given birth to three children was free from hard labor the rest of her life; if she had four she became wholly free.

The slave traffic was very active over all the imperial Roman world during the whole period of its existence, and was the most lucrative branch of commerce. It was also strictly adjusted by police regulations.

Augustus likewise made efforts to morally re-invigorate, so to speak, the decaying oligarchy; but this attempt was even more unsuccessful than the former. Every person who is even slightly acquainted with history must be familiar with the absolute degradation of the oligarchs, capitalists, and rich slaveholders of imperial Rome. Tiberius despised them and tyrannized over them with a cold-blooded and contemptuous cruelty only equalled by the manner in which they crushed their chattels, or the populace of Rome, whom they had impoverished and degraded. For then, as for centuries before, the oligarchy looked with as much contempt on the working-classes as the modern slave-drivers do on "greasy mechanics." But, in the eye of history and humanity, it is the "greasy mechanics" and "small-fisted farmers" of the free states who are the glorious lights which redeem the dark side of American polity as embodied in the slave-driving chivalry.

In fact, the Roman oligarchs were far more degraded than their chattels. *"Turpis adulatio Senatus,"* said Tacitus; and the names of Druses, Germanicus, Britannicus, Chærea, Trasea, and a few others, can never redeem the infamy of a whole community.

The numbers of slaves owned by the wealthy, was, as it were, proportionate to their degradation. Athenæus says that some rich men had from ten to twenty thousand slaves, and the statement is confirmed by Seneca. Cæcilius Isidorus, a rich *particulier* living under Augustus, lost a great part of his fortune in the civil wars, and yet left by will 4116 chattels; Elius Proculus, on his estates in Liguria, had two thousand slaves able to bear arms; Scaurus, a wealthy senator, owned 4116 chattels, exclusive of shepherds and tillers; Eumolpus, a simple citizen-not one of the oligarchs or F.F.V.'s of that time, but rather a *parvenu* —had so large a number of slaves on his estates in Numidia, that with an army of them he could have stormed and taken the city of Carthage, which, although reduced from its former grandeur, was still among the first cities of Africa. Under Nero, half of Africa was owned by six slaveholders: Nero slaughtered them and inherited their estates.

Such was the rapidly developed internal condition of the Roman state when Pliny dolefully exclaimed: *"Latifundi perdidere Italiam moxque provincias:"* "Large extended estates (cultivated by slaves), ruined Italy, and soon after the provinces," as even Spain and Gaul were quickly devoured by the large slaveholders.

The condition and treatment of the slaves inspired pity even in a Claudius. He prohibited the custom of starving to death the old and disabled slaves, who had generally been exposed on an island in the Tiber, upon which was a temple of Esculapius. By the Claudian edict, such exposition was equivalent to emancipation. Even Nero had some pity for the slaves, though he had none for their masters. The emperors were terrified at the increased ravages of slavery, which spread in continually wider and wider circles over Gaul and Spain as well as in Africa and in the east. Edicts were issued by several emperors-as Adrian and the Antonines-designed to stay the spread of slavery and alleviate the condition of the chattels. These edicts encouraged manumissions either absolute and immediate, or gradual, and conferred the same municipal rights as were enjoyed by the enfranchised. The *latifundia*, or large estates, nevertheless, still increased their size; and the condition and relations of landed property required new laws and new legal definitions, which were gradually introduced into the *jus civile*. First in order were the common usages of the people, and then the legalization of their customs. Thus it is not till toward the end of the second Christian century that there are found in the Roman law definitions of slaves as persons attached perpetually to the soil. But their classification was so complicated, that it becomes difficult, if not impossible, to define distinctly the various grades, or to exhibit clearly the features in which one differs from another. The necessities of the imperial treasury were probably the cause of such divisions as those of *adscriptitii, censiti, perpetui, conditionales, coloni, inquilini* —both of old republican origin —*simplices, originarii, homologi, tributari, addicti glebæ, agricolæ, aratores, rustici actores, etc.* In course of time, also, all these names were merged under the general denomination of serfs, which again assumed various degrees of oppression and servitude.

Augustus is proverbially said to have pacified the world; and indeed, with few exceptions, the Roman empire enjoyed internal peace during the first two Christian centuries. But under Claudius, during the war with Tiridates of Pontus, the entire population of some of the captured cities was sold into slavery, as were also one hundred thousand Jews, when Jerusalem fell under Vespasian. There were now, however, no more rich cities or cultivated countries to be conquered, no peoples to be enslaved by millions, as there had been under the republic; wars now were waged only on the outskirts of the empire, and generally with barbarous nations. Prisoners of war, captives and subdued barbarians, were no longer sold into slavery, but the emperors colonized the waste lands with them. They thus attempted to repeople Italy and the provinces, and to revive the ancient mode of rural economy, as also to increase the revenue of the imperial treasury. Such colonizations were frequent after the time of Marcus Aurelius. But all this could not stop the growth of the social cancer. Chattelhood, encouraged, as will be shown by political slavery and taxations, was wildly rampant, and overleaped every barrier to its progress which the emperors attempted to raise.

During the whole epoch of the growth and maturity of domestic slavery in Rome, no one of her moralists, philosophers, poets, priests or satirists ever preached or sang of the idyllic beauties of slavery; none of her statesmen considered it as the foundation, corner-stone or cement of society or of the empire, or even as "ennobling"[15] to the slaveholder, and orations and discourses in exaltation of human bondage were unknown. Pliny, Seneca and Plutarch only spoke of it in extenuating language.

The Roman jurisconsult of the better times of the empire crystallized into legal form the sense of justice and equity inherent in the Roman, nay, in human society. He expounded the law for the *de facto* existing society, and therefore generally in favor of the owner, slaveholder, etc., and against the thing, the *res*, which was the chattel. The object of the Roman law was only to regulate existing relations, and such was domestic slavery. But with all its unbending severity, the Roman law, through the conscientious voice of the Roman jurisconsult, declared slavery a condition, *"qua quis dominio alieno contra naturam subiicitur,"* and rarely missed an occasion to favor the slave, to alleviate his status, and to facilitate his emancipation. No clause or decision of the law re-enslaved, in any case, the chattel once emancipated. Even if a will provided for the emancipation of a slave in terms like these: "I will and command that my slave A becomes free; but upon condition that he live with my son, and if he refuses or neglects to do this he returns to slavery," the law decided, that "A, being emancipated by the first paragraph of the will, cannot be re-enslaved by the subsequent conditional paragraph; therefore A is free, and he may or may not fulfil the condition."

The child also followed the condition of the mother when born from illicit intercourse, *nisi lex specialis alius inducit*. If the father was a slave and the mother a free woman, the child was free, *quia non debet calamitas matris ei noceri qui in utero est* —"the misfortune of the mother shall not bear on the product of the womb." A change of the status of the mother from liberty to slavery during pregnancy was always construed favorably to the child, who thus might be born free if the mother was free for even the shortest time during the period of pregnancy.

Under the emperors, freemen began to sell themselves into slavery —a thing unknown during the existence of the republic. But a freeman who sold himself into slavery, if afterward manumitted, could not become again a full citizen. And whoever was once emancipated could on no pretence be re-enslaved, under penalty of death.

Modern pro-slavery legislators and jurisconsults boldly overthrow all these Roman ideas of justice and equity.

The law established various *just* causes for emancipation. Among these were, natural relationships, as children, brothers, sisters, mothers, cousins, grandparents, etc., when slaves; and whoever *ad impudicitiam turpemque violationem servos compellat*, lost his *potestas*, or power, over the slave.

These facilities for emancipation operated principally in favor of the urban chattels, or those of the household proper, and also rural overseers, but were rarely applied to the rural slaves; consequently, during the most brilliant period of the existence of the empire, the cities were filled with enfranchised slaves of various kinds and various nations. The country, too, was altogether abandoned by the slaveholders, who lived and rioted in the imperial city. Most of these emancipated slaves, as also, indeed, many of the free-born citizens, finally lost their liberty by the operation of those causes which, notwithstanding emancipations and state colonizations, continually increased the *latifundia* or large estates, and transformed into bondmen the freeholders as well as those who rented land from the state or from private individuals.

The civil administration of the Roman empire, heathen and Christian, down to its last agonies in Constantinople, may be very briefly summed up: it was *fiscality*. Every administrative measure aimed at replenishing the imperial exchequer. The imperial treasury was bottomless, and its owners cold, rapacious, cruel and insatiable. All the colonizations of free laborers had for their single aim but to increase the income of the state; and tributes and taxations of every conceivable kind were imposed, first upon the provinces, and in course of time, on Italy itself. These, of course, were principally supplied by the laboring classes in the cities and on the lands. The rapacity of the state was heightened also by the individual greed of the magistrates, from the prefects down to the meanest military or political official or tax-gatherer; indeed, locusts more destructive than the Roman officials never devoured the fruits of toil or the accumulations of industry. These fiscal measures and lawless extortions, fostered chattelhood almost as much as wars and conquests had formerly done.

The *inquilini* and *coloni* of the last century of the republic were free, rent-paying farmers (who paid the rent in money), or free laborers. When, after the time of Sylla, the republican oligarchs partially enslaved these farmers, the rent had to be paid in kind, in sign of dependence, if not of absolute bondage. The colonists settled by the emperors also had to pay tribute and submit to various other servitudes; and thus the once free colonists were, by a slow but uninterrupted process, transformed into bondmen, serfs and slaves. As in the last days of the republic, so under Augustus and his successors, the free yeoman or colonist, in order to avoid being violently expelled from his homestead and shut up in the *ergastulum* with the chattels, frequently sold himself and his little property, on certain conditions, to the rich and powerful slaveholder, and thus secured patronage and protection. In proportion as exaction, oppression and lawlessness increased under the emperors, so also did the forced or voluntary submission of colonists to influential slaveholders. As the imperial tax-gatherer was wont to sell the children of the poor for tax or tribute, the peasant often preferred to become a slave in order to obtain protection from his master, who became responsible to the treasury for the taxes of the bondman and his lands. Frequently whole villages of colonists thus gave up their rights for the sake of patronage and protection.

The exchequer had a roll inscribed with the names of all the colonists on the domains belonging to the state, the cities, or to private individuals. From this census for taxation was derived the legal designation, and afterward the condition of *adscriptus*. And the imperial government, whose sole object was to gather taxes and have responsible tax-payers, had little if any objection to this transformation of colonists and their homesteads into the bondmen of the rich. The change was not made at once by any special law,[16] but was brought about by the slow progress of social decomposition. When the serfdom of the colonists first became an object of jurisprudence —a little before and under Theodosius-it had already existed as a fact; and *ex facto nascitur jus* was an old axiom of the civil law. By and by slaves proper-that is, movable chattels, not persons attached to the soil-both in the city and on the lands, were taxed on the plantation roll; and Constantine prohibited the sale of chattels from one province to another, most probably with the view of facilitating their control by the tax-gatherer.

Rapacious taxation, the first outgrowth of imperial despotism which was originated by the slaveholders, forced into the grip of the oligarch all that remained of free soil and independent labor, or what was intended to be such by the colonizing emperors. The same cause also disorganized the ancient municipal regime in the cities of Italy and throughout the Roman world.

The *curia* of Italian cities, and afterward of all other cities privileged with Italian law, constituted the body politic of each municipality. The most influential and wealthy citizens, therefore, were *curiales*; next to them were *municipes*, common burghers, small traders, etc.; then clients, free plebeian proletarians, the enfranchised, etc. The *decurions* or city senate, and other dignitaries called patrons, protectors, etc., administered the affairs of the city; these and all other offices were light and honorable while the cities were flourishing, as in the first two centuries of the empire; but even then, various legal immunities released *curiales* from performing public municipal service. During the peace enjoyed by the Roman world in the early times of the empire, the taxes, tolls, excises, *venalicium*, etc., imposed on Italianized cities, were moderate. These cities were then rich; they accumulated and loaned capital; they owned slaves and extensive domains. By means of their slaves they erected those public edifices and monuments whose splendor rivalled those of Rome and whose ruins are still in many places preserved; and the administration of the revenues and the honors of the city were in the control of rich oligarchs and slaveholders. The same accumulation of wealth in the hands of a few, existed in the cities as in the country, as the same oligarchs generally lived in the city, and indeed necessarily belonged to some *municipium*; for in the Roman world the whole political and civic status was exclusively embodied in and bestowed on the city; and the country, as such, had no political or civil significance.

Thus, even during the most brilliant periods, the numerous free persons in the cities became more and more impoverished, and lived by *panem et circenses*, as in Rome. Under this deceitful glitter, the disease slowly undermined the prosperity of the cities, and the first shock revealed the terrible reality. Soon fiscal rapacity seized hold of every thing both in the Italian and Italianized cities. Not only the poorer classes but even the wealthy began to feel it. One after another the cities lost their domains and their treasure, and thus lost the means to sustain their internal administration. With the growing imperial rapacity increased also the danger and the difficulties of public office, as the *decurions* and other officials were responsible to the imperial treasury for all the taxes and imposts levied upon the city. The rich men, patrons, etc., now used extensively their right of exemption from office, and excused themselves from public service in proportion as the fiscal pressure increased, and as they found it more lucrative to profit from general calamities than to attempt to avert them. Besides, taxes for the central exchequer were to be imposed and levied as well as taxes for the local administration of the cities. All this finally almost entirely crushed the impoverished burghers, and in the second century large numbers of burghers were inscribed in the *curia*. First the poorer shopkeepers, artisans, and small property holders, and then almost all the *viles*, with the exception of the *infames* —that is, those who at any time had undergone any infamous condemnation-became *curiales*. Taxes on lands, houses, and slaves, and also on persons (*per capita*), increased almost daily, and were imposed under various guises and new names. All handicraftsmen, tradesmen, and merchants, had to pay special taxes, and the poorest plebeian had to pay a *capitatio* or *illatio*. When the cities had thus been reduced to poverty, and were obliged to tax themselves heavily to sustain their existence, the severest of all labor was to be a city official, and every one tried to avoid public honors, as even to be a *curialis* was considered a heavy calamity. The surplus of the poor free population, no longer supported by the magistrates or *decuriones*, abandoned the cities and became colonists on the imperial domains, on the remaining city domains, or on private lands; and there sank deeper and deeper into the mire of slavery. Soon the *curiales* began to follow the plebeians, in order to escape from their privileges and dignities. With this, however, an imperial edict interfered, and small proprietors, curiales, etc., were prohibited from selling their property. The eventual acquirer of such property was made *ipso facto* curial, and responsible for both past and current taxes, and the other exactions and servitudes imposed. The law put various other impediments on the personal liberty of poor but taxable curiales: they became bondmen of the state or of their own municipality; they could not change their residence, and suffered innumerable annoyances. The curiales, thus goaded, often preferred even the hateful military service on the utmost frontiers of the empire: they voluntarily entered the legions, in order to be exempted from taxation and the grip of the imperial and municipal tax-gatherer. More of them, however, chose rather to seek patrons, and became bondmen to the rich, the slaveholders, and exempted persons, giving both themselves and their property to their protectors. Thus frequently the impoverished descendants of former *honoratiores* became first bondmen and then slaves. During that long epoch of grinding oppression and taxation, the division and subdivision of the community into classes and grades originated. This classification was based on pursuits and occupations, and also according to the imposts levied on each class, from the magnate-as the rich social successors of the oligarchs were now called-down to the lowest laborer and chattel. Finally, the whole property in the Roman world-the country, the city, the lands, houses, and slaves-was centred in the hands of a few magnates, who owned incalculable numbers of colonists, bondmen, serfs, and chattels.

The famous Roman legions were recruited from yeomen, plebeians, workmen and colonists; in one word, from the free population. When freemen diminished, foreigners and barbarians were hired and enrolled. Sylla's military murderers were in great part Spanish Celts; and after Sylla and Marius, foreigners entered more and more into the composition of the Roman armies. Caligula had a kind of body-guard composed of Germans; and soon all the nations conquered by Rome were represented, not only in the armies, but even under the imperial canopy. Then arose the intestine wars for imperial power carried on by pretenders, each *proclaimed* by some province or legion. These wars resulted in slaughter, devastation, ruin and universal misery; and thus enlarged the number of slaves, and powerfully revived the slave traffic, which survived the downfall of heathenism and the Roman world.

Domestic slavery, acting through long centuries, brought about a thoroughly diseased and depraved condition of society, which, in turn, reacted upon its producing cause, exacerbating and intensifying it. The result was, that domestic slavery quite overmastered the ancient Roman world. At the melancholy period of Rome's disruption, the high-souled, patriotic citizen-that compact and columnar type of character-had become quite extinct, and in his place were large slave-owners, slave-drivers, and slave-traders. The masters and protectors of Rome were for-eigners and barbarians. The slaveholders could not defend the empire, and beneath them was a degraded population of so-called freemen, and millions of serfs and slaves, all of them without a spark of love for their country, and destitute even of material incitements to urge them to defend their homes or uphold the existing condition of society. None of them had any interest to sustain their slaveholding masters or the fiscality of the empire; and at times the lower classes, the slaves especially, even joined the invaders. Thus, when Alaric appeared before Rome, over forty thousand slaves joined his camp.

Such was the condition of the Roman world and its western provinces, Spain and Gaul, when the avalanche from the north burst upon it with its torrent of invaders. The oligarchic slaveholders, having destroyed the republic, transmitted to the Cæsars a society which had through their means become utterly degenerate and depraved. The emperors, in their turn, transmitted to the new era a world putrescent with domestic slavery. Often does a virus eat its way so deeply into a healthy organism, as to change its very character and the conditions of its existence. Then the morbid disorganization becomes an apparently normal condition, until finally life is altogether extinct. Such was the effect of chattelhood on the Roman world, and especially on Italy, which was the soul and centre of the system. Nor does it require any great apprehension to see how the tragic analogy holds in the case of the Southern States of the North American confederacy.

XIV. Christianity: Its Churches and Creeds

AUTHORITIES:

General History, Ecclesiastical History, Councils, Bulls, etc.

Christianity appeared for the purpose of effecting a regeneration in man's moral nature; this necessarily included also his social regeneration.

The primitive Christians, apostles, and martyrs, by their words, actions, and death, taught charity, brotherly love, and equality before God; and thus slowly but powerfully undermined slavery. They consoled in every possible way their lowly and suffering brethren, and tried to inspire the slaveholders with feelings of charity and benevolence toward their bondmen; but as the apostles did not attack any prevalent social or political evil, nay, even seemed to countenance, by their silent recognition or their advice, the existing imperial despotism, so, for obvious reasons, they could not directly attack domestic slavery nor proclaim universal emancipation. They preached to slaves and slaveholders, made converts from both, and considered and treated both as equal before God and the law. The few words of apostolic consolation which have been transmitted to us as referring especially to chattels, logically and morally contain a condemnation of slavery, for it is only misfortune and evil that inspire pity or require consolation. So that the apostles and primitive Christians, by advising slaves to bear their yoke patiently, thereby proclaimed slavery to be an evil, like any of the sufferings, losses, or misfortunes of life.

When, under Constantine, Christianity was embodied in a national ecclesiasticism, the Church watched more directly over the condition of the slaves. In various ways it tried to alleviate their condition and effect their manumission; and this it urged the more earnestly as the Christians belonged mostly to the poorer classes, and also numerous serfs and slaves.

But the Church had now become a material fact, and henceforward, beside its legitimate moral aims, it had also worldly and selfish desires. It received imperial and private donations, became a large proprietor of lands, and therefore also a holder of slaves and serfs. It could therefore take no distinct interest in emancipation, but nevertheless still continued to inspire slaveholders with a milder spirit, and tried to prevent, as far as possible, the slave traffic, at least in Christian chattels.

None of the apostles, fathers, confessors, or martyrs of the Church ever affirmed slavery to be a moral and divine institution, or ever attempted to justify it in any way. These primitive Christians and holy fathers never once thought to refer to the curse of Noah as a justification of slavery. The Biblical story of Noah and his curse was first dragged into this question by the feudalized mediæval clergy, to justify the enslavement, not of black Africans but of white Europeans, among whom, undoubtedly, were the ancestors of many blatant American supporters of the divine origin, on Biblical authority, of slavery.

When the Roman empire was broken in pieces by the northern invaders, the body of the Roman Church and clergy belonged to the subdued and enslaved race. The Franks, Northmen, and Anglo-Saxons were then altogether heathen; but many of the invaders-as the Visigoths and Ostrogoths, the Vandals, Burgundians, Heruli, and Longobards-were Christians; but, being Arians (Unitarians), they were enemies of the Trinitarians, and treated the Roman clergy as they did the rest of the subdued population. The Roman clergy, however, finally succeeded in superseding the Arian dogmas by their own, and they then constituted the sole expounders of Christian doctrine. Moved then by the Christian spirit, as well as by consanguinity with the enslaved population, they never failed to impress on the conquerors, whether heathen or Christian, their duties toward their slaves. They also continued to promote manumissions by declaring them meritorious before God. These manumissions were performed at the sacred altar with all the pomp and impressive rites of the Church, and were often extorted from the slaveholding barbarian in his last agonies.

As before, so during the first centuries of the Germanic settlements of Western and Southern Europe, the Church never recognized the right of one man to enslave another; but rather through the voice of Gregory the Great, bishop, pope, or saint, reaffirmed the ancient axiom of the Roman jurist: *"Homines quos ab initio natura creavit liberos-et jus gentium jugo substituit servitutis."* The efforts of Gregory the Great, as also those of his predecessors and successors, were directed toward stopping the infamous slave traffic, first in Christian slaves, and then in Jews, Mussulmans, and all heathen. The Roman Church and its leaders unceasingly condemned the slave-trade, and the popes menaced with excommunication the traffickers in Mussulman prisoners in Rome, Lyons, Venice, etc., as also those Germans who afterward, in the ninth, tenth, and eleventh centuries, enslaved the prisoners of war which they made among the Slavonic tribes, Christian and heathen. The popes have likewise perpetually condemned the African or negro slave-trade, from its beginning down to the present day. Gregory XVI. interdicts "all ecclesiastics from venturing to maintain *that this traffic in blacks* is permitted under any pretext whatsoever;" and prohibits "teaching in public or in private, in any way whatever, any thing contrary to this apostolic letter." Explicit words of this tenor, coming from the pope, were generally considered as expressing the spirit of the Papal Church. In the Roman, as in all other churches and sects, however, both clergy and laity were wont to interpret all such mandates according to their own convenience.

For reasons formerly alluded to, the various national ecclesiastical councils held in countries politically reconstructed by German invaders-as Spain, France, and England-repeatedly and explicitly legislated on slavery. These councils had it constantly in view to moderate the general treatment of slaves and bondmen, and to prevent mutilation and other cruel modes of punishment. The churches were proclaimed inviolable places of refuge for fugitive slaves, and while emancipation was urged as meritorious, the enslavement of freemen was visited with excommunication.

Soon, however, the Church, that is, the priesthood and hierarchy, came to form an integral part of the feudal system. The higher clergy shared the public spoils, and had fiefs and other estates stocked with serfs and chattels. Then the fervor for emancipation abated; nevertheless, the clergy generally recommended a humane treatment of the enslaved. The Irish clergy and councils perhaps proved themselves the most disinterested at that early mediæval epoch: they were the "underground railroad" of the period-assisting in the escape of slaves from bondage; and a council held in Armagh in 1172, gave *liberty* to all *English* (that is, Saxon) slaves in Ireland. Nowadays, on the contrary, the immense majority of the Irish Roman clergy on this continent support and sanction chattel slavery.

In the course of time the clerical hierarchies, monasteries, etc., inoculated with the feudal and baronial spirit, became as zealous for the preservation of even the most revolting forms of servitude imposed upon the bondmen, as the most rapacious lay barons could possibly have been. Nowhere did the clergy raise its voice for either a total or a partial abolition of bondage.

Serfdom, which had long previously vanished from Italy, was, at the appearance of Luther, on the point of dissolution in England. The father of the religious reformation of Germany rather avoided blending social with spiritual reform; but the French and Swiss reformers, as well as the anabaptists and other sects, kept especially in view the amelioration of the condition of the oppressed masses. In general, the great movements for a freer spiritual activity which characterized the sixteenth century, contributed to promote the emancipation of serfs: and this first by purifying and elevating the public conscience, and then by bringing about the secularization of church property. The state, on becoming the heir of the clergy, was everywhere foremost in abolishing servitude: the ecclesiastical corporation, on the other hand, never labored for its abolition.

Among the various religious bodies-the Quakers and the modern Unitarians excepted-the absoluteness of Christian doctrine and morals has always been greatly modified by worldly interests. Not the Episcopal nor Scottish churches, nor indeed any other denomination, can claim the merit of having begotten the noble sentiment so universal in England on the subject of human bondage. The Roman clergy continues, as it always has done, to oscillate between duty and interest; and the various Protestant sects do the same. And it is a significant feature that in the American Union almost every religious denomination has its pro-slavery and its anti-slavery factions.

XV. Gauls

AUTHORITIES:

Cæsar, Dieffenbach, Picot, Amadee Thierry, etc.

The Gauls (*Gadhels, Gaels* or *Gals*), a branch of the Aryas, were the first historic race which peopled Central and Western Europe. It is supposed that the Gauls (afterward wrongly called Kelts) emigrated from Asia to Europe before the Greeks, Latins, or Slavonians, as undoubtedly they did long previous to the Teutons or Germans. Already, in prehistoric times, from the regions of the Danube to the Atlantic, on the Alps and the Pyrenees as well as on the British and Irish islands, these first wanderers left their marks in the names of rivers and mountains. Gallia (Gaul) finally became their home, and from thence they repeatedly issued forth and shook the ancient world, ravaged Greece and extended their empire to Asia Minor on the east, and Italy on the south. They burnt republican Rome in its very infancy, and for centuries the Roman republic struggled for life and death with them, until they were finally subdued by Cæsar.

The whole of Gaul was occupied by tribes more or less consanguineous, and their internal social organization was in many respects similar. Cæsar, in his bird's-eye view, says that the two dominant classes were the druids and nobles, while under them were the *"plebs, pœne servorem habetur loco, quæ per nihil audet et nullo adhibitur consiglio."* This only explains the absence or perhaps dormancy of political rights. *"Plerique* (not *all*, it will be noticed, but *many*, and these mainly such as had suffered reverses of fortune) *sesse in servitutem* DICANT *nobilibus-in hos eadem omnia sunt jura quæ dominis in servis."* This latter phrase only means that certain relations between the chief and his dependents were similar to those of master and chattel-being the only form of servitude known to Cæsar, who did not understand the tribal organization on which the authority of the chief was based.

Parke Godwin, in his highly elaborate and valuable History of France, says very justly that "the Gallic society was a mere conglomeration of chieftains and followers." After giving a picture of Gallic family life and exhibiting the nature of the chieftain's power and functions, that eminent writer thus continues: "The other members of the clan consisted of a number of dependents in various degrees of subordination, and of adherents whose ties were more or less voluntary." Among the dependents were "bondmen (attached to the soil), debtor-bondmen, *obaerati*, strangers found in the country without a protector or lord, and slaves, captives of war or purchased in the open market." Thus far Parke Godwin.

Slaves, if indeed such existed among the Gauls at the time of Cæsar, were certainly exceedingly limited in number, and chattelhood was not an inherent condition of any part of the people. In his history of his long wars with the Gauls, Cæsar makes no allusion to a slave-element in the population-an omission which shows how insignificant it must have been.

The commercial relations of the Gauls with the Phœnicians and with the Greek colony of Massilia, or Marseilles, probably tended to encourage slavery among them. But although our knowledge of their internal relations and domestic economy is very scanty, there are a few facts which prove that domestic slavery was hardly even in an embryonic stage at the epoch when the Gauls, by their contact with Rome and Cæsar, entered the general current of history. The Massaliotes (or colonists established at Marseilles), trafficked in slaves. They also had them in their houses, but did not employ them on lands situated beyond the precincts of the city. For field laborers they hired the Ligurians, who, at given seasons, descended with their wives from the mountains and worked for wages. Lands belonging to Gallic clans or districts were no more worked by slave labor than were the fields of the Massaliotes. Even in the households of the chieftains or nobles, domestic slavery, if it existed, must have been hidden from sight. Possidonius, tutor of Pompey, Cicero, and other eminent Romans, gives a description of the mode of life and domestic customs of the Gauls, in whose country he travelled. He observed, that at their luxurious feasts the guests were served by the children of the family, instead of domestic slaves; which fact authorizes the conclusion that the number of chattels was very small, and that they had no place in family life.

Gallic slaves consisted of criminals, vagabonds, foreigners imported from Massilia, and prisoners of war principally made from nations beyond the Alps and the Rhine. Even after the invasion of the Kimbri and Belgæ, Gaul was inhabited by tribes more or less akin to each other. It was therefore the theatre of almost uninterrupted domestic war between tribes and federations. But when one tribe was conquered by another, the subject people and those who escaped the fury of battle were not reduced to slavery, but simply became tributary, and received their laws from the conqueror. Exceptions to this rule must have been exceedingly rare. If an invading tribe was subdued, it received lands and was obliged to settle among the conquerors. The founders of Rome, as we saw (see "Romans: Republicans"), acted in a similar manner. Prisoners of war were absorbed into the clan, and were held, perhaps exclusively by the chieftain, in the condition of serfs bound to the soil, but not as chattels or marketable objects; and they were neither deprived of personality nor the rights of family.

The arable lands, forests, and pasturages were owned by the clan collectively-the chiefs, of course, receiving the lion's share when distributed for cultivation; and each clan lived on its own lands. These agricultural clansmen it was who constituted the terrible armies which, under various Brenni (chiefs, leaders, kings), so often terrified and scourged almost the whole known world.

With the increase of the wealth and power of the chieftains, their relations with the poorer clansmen became more aggressive, and the lands were held by the latter under conditions more and more onerous. But when Cæsar invaded Gaul, no large estates (*latifundia*) existed, and the soil was in the hands of a numerous peasantry inspired with patriotism and love of independence. This peasantry flocked to the standard of Vercingetorix, and, to the last, sustained him in his deadly struggle against Cæsar.

The living acoustic telegraph used by the Gauls during the wars with Cæsar is another proof that great estates did not exist in Gaul, and that the soil was tilled by freemen possessed of homesteads: for each peasant, from the limit of his homestead, shouted the news to his next neighbor, he to the next, and so on; and thus intelligence was swiftly carried hundreds of miles even during the shortest day of the year. An important event occurring in any one tribe was thus spread in a twinkling all over Gaul. Now, if the country had been divided into large estates worked by slaves, such a mode of communication would of course have been impossible.

As the clans and their land were governed by chieftains and nobles, so also were the cities under oligarchic rule. The free population in the cities had no independent rights, and was obliged to have patrons. The poor, the defenceless, and even the artisans, willingly enrolled themselves for life under the clientship of the powerful nobility, depending on them as the rural clansmen depended upon the chieftains or rural nobles. But the condition of a client in the city was not hereditary or transmissible, as was clanship in the country. The *family* of the client held no relations of dependency upon the patron; and a son was not bound by obligations contracted by his father. When the patron died, the bonds of his clients were severed, and they were free to select another patron.

Such were the relations between the chieftains and clansmen, between the nobility and the people, between the soil and its tiller, between client and patron, when the Romans commenced the conquest of Gaul. Impoverishment, debts contracted to their chiefs, and exactions of one kind and another, may have transformed many independent clansmen into partial bondmen; but they always preserved their family and village rights.

After the numerous evidences already pointed out in the history of the Greeks and Romans, it is unnecessary here to show how similar morbid causes produced correspondingly destructive effects in the crude civilization and social condition of the Gauls. The development of these germs brought the Gauls almost to serfdom, if not yet to chattelhood, at the same time degrading the character of the oligarchs-future slaveholders-to the extent described by Cæsar. This perversion of the internal economy of the Gauls prepared them for domestic slavery. Thus often an insignificant derangement in the human economy, or a trifling lesion in its organism, may find its ultimate result only in permanent disorganization or in *death*.

The Roman conquest and the subsequent oppressive administration, contributed to establish the same relations between the population in Gaul as existed in Italy and Spain, and which have been already described. The city (*municipium*) became all and every thing; the clan, the district, the country nothing. The former chiefs of the clans became the senators of their respective centres. The imperial Roman administration favored the concentration of landed estates into a few hands, and consequently the impoverishment of small landholders and free laborers and operatives of every kind; and thereby greatly increased the growth of slavery. The collective ownership of the land by the clan and its chiefs became wholly transformed into the individual property of the chief, who was now also a municipal senator or magnate. A striking analogy to this is found in the Highlands of Scotland, which, in the same way have become the property of a few powerful families. The Gallic clansmen before being transformed into chattels, first became tenants (*coloni*) —similar to those in imperial Italy-of their chiefs (or *tierns*), who, on becoming senators, lived in the cities, and were surrounded, not by clients and clansmen, but by slaves. The estates now began to be worked by bondmen and chattels, and thus a servile population succeeded to the free and sturdy yeomanry of ancient times.

Not without a struggle, however, was this accomplished. The oppressive taxation, the tyranny of the domestic oligarchs, and the devastations committed by barbarians-the vanguards of the future destroyers of the Roman empire-generated in the third century the repeated insurrections of the *Bagaudes* (the Gallic name for *insurgent*), that is, of the peasantry against the cities. All the oppressed small land-owners, tenants, serfs and slaves united in these insurrections.

The slave traffic was now very brisk. The Roman prefects, tribunes, etc., sold the prisoners of war made in the German invasions; while the Germans, in their turn, when successful, carried away or sold their booty to the human traffickers from various regions. Thus Aurelian, who was a military tribune previous to becoming emperor, sold several hundred Franks, Suevians, etc., probably in the city of Maguncia (Mayence). Soon the forays became more and more destructive, and for several centuries invasion succeeded invasion until the impoverishment and ruin of the people were accomplished. The issue of a long train of interacting social circumstances was the same in Gaul as in Italy: senators and oligarchs owned the lands and the cities, and proudly domineered, while the rest of the population sank into tenants, serfs, and bondmen, and most of them into chattels. These last had, of course, nothing to defend against the invaders, who even at times in many ways alleviated their condition: therefore the invaders were often received with open arms by the enslaved populations. When the destroyers of the Roman rule over Gaul finally settled therein, many of the nobles and rich magnates understood how to ingratiate themselves with their new masters, and thus shared in their spoils of lands and slaves. By far the greater number, however, were themselves ruined and enslaved.

In Gaul, as over the whole ancient and Roman world, not the slaveholders but their slaves survived the general destruction, nay, finally stepped into the places once occupied by their enslavers and masters.

XVI. Germans

AUTHORITIES:

Tacitus, Codex Legum Antiquorum Barbarorum, Jacob Grimm, Mentzel, Wirth, Puetter, Zimmerman, etc.

The Germans, in all probability, were the last of the Aryan stock who immigrated into Europe. History first discovers them finally settled in central Europe; and for how long a time they had previously roamed in the primitive forests of these regions it is impossible to conjecture. With the exception of the left bank of the Rhine, Switzerland, and the northern slopes of the Tyrolean Alps-which regions, in the course of centuries were conquered from various Keltic tribes-the Germany proper of to-day is about the same as when Cæsar met the barbarians on the Rhine. Then the Germans were rude savages, with but little agriculture; living on milk, cheese, and flesh; and their condition was in many respects similar, perhaps even inferior, to that of the Tartars, Kalmucks, and Bashkirs, who still rove over northern and central Asia.

Neither clanship nor patriarchate existed among the Germans, but the rule of individual will strengthened by the family ties. Divided into numerous tribes, the Germans seem to have spent many centuries in hunting the wild beasts of their primitive forests, and in making war upon each other. Most probably these almost uninterrupted domestic wars created and developed aristocracy and slavery, both of which were firmly established among the Germans when they first appear on the record of history. Among the European descendants of the Aryas, the primitive Germans reflect most strikingly the Euphratic story of Nimrod, "the strong," "the hunter," subduing the feeble and preying on his person and labor. A bitter hatred between the tribes prevailed from time immemorial; and consequently feuds and wars were perpetual. The conquered was compelled to labor for the conqueror; and thus originated, very probably, bondage and domestic slavery, as well as the aristocratic contempt which the fighting part of the population had for the subdued and enslaved laborers of a tribe. When one German tribe subdued another, the victors either seized on the lands of the conquered and settled thereon, transforming the former occupants into bondmen; or, if they did not settle among the subdued, they made them tributaries, carrying away a certain portion of the population as slaves. Thus the Germans, in their wild forests, were mainly divided into two great social elements-the freemen, or nobles, possessed of all rights, and the bondmen possessed of none. But all, free and slave, were of kindred race and lineage.

All the German dialects have a specific denomination for the chattel. *Schalch, scalch, schalk,* is the word for slave, and *seneschalk* for the overseer. Afterward, in mediæval times, *seneschalk* was an office, dignity, or title.

Besides wars and conquests, there were other sources which fed and sustained slavery: thus certain crimes were punished with slavery, and even freemen gambled away their liberty —a custom found among no other race or nation; a freeman, likewise, could at any time sell himself into slavery. Any one condemned to compound in money for murder or any other offence, if he had no money, gave himself as a slave into the hands of the family or individual whom he had offended, or to the man who loaned him money to pay the composition. The *schalks* were more absolutely in the power of their master than were the Roman slaves under the empire, or even, if possible, than the chattels of the American slave states. Although Tacitus says that masters killed their slaves only when intoxicated or otherwise maddened with passion, the barbarian codes and other historic evidence show that the *schalks* were treated with the utmost cruelty, and even subject to be maimed in various ways. Some historians who hold up the Germans as models of social and civic virtue, attribute this cruelty to their contact with the Romans, whose example they followed. But the influence of Roman polity on Germany began only toward the end of the fourth century; and many of the northern tribes, as the Saxons, Frisians, etc., did not come under the influence of Roman, Christian, or any foreign civilization till about the eighth century. Some of these barbarian codes were written when the barbarians had settled on the Roman ruins; then, undoubtedly, they incorporated some Roman ideas, and contained laws bearing on existing relations; but still they were principally the embodiment of their own immemorial usages. The Visigothic code, for instance, was written very soon after they settled in Gaul and Spain, long before the destruction of the Western empire, and consequently could not have been seriously influenced by the legal conceptions or customs of Rome.

Tacitus says that little difference existed between the mode of life of masters and slaves: *Inter eadem pecora in eadem humo degunt.* At the time of Diodorus Siculus, youthful male and female *schalks* served at the tables of masters, who were always willing to sell them for a jug of wine.

In this primitive epoch of German historical existence, the pride of blood and descent seems to have been deeply ingrained in the German mind; and there was a strong aversion against corrupting the lineage by intermarriage with a *schalk* man or woman, even although they were of the same race and family. Among the Saxons immemorial custom even punished a *mesalliance* with death. Thus the very ancestors of many American slaveholders, now so proud of their Saxon blood, were considered unworthy of marriage with their masters. But concubinage with slave women was then common (as it now is in the South), whatever Tacitus may say concerning German conjugal fidelity. The bastards of parents one free the other slave, became serfs to the soil. If a freeman married a slave woman, their children were *schalks*, and sometimes the father even was reduced to slavery. A free woman marrying a slave, might be killed by her parents or became a slave of the king-when the Germans had kings in their new, post-Roman monarchies. Most of these cruel legal customs, and many others found in the codes, belong to the heathen epoch, to the period of pure Germanic existence unadulterated by contact with the corruptions of civilized life. They prove how deep was the Germanic contempt for the ignoble or unfortunate among their own brethren; they show also the very ancient appearance of slavery among them, and its violent and criminal origin, like that of slavery always and everywhere.

Ancient usages and laws regulating inheritance perpetuate themselves remarkably among peoples and nations. From their forests the Germans transplanted the right of primogeniture over Europe. The land was given to the males, while the daughters received the movables, *mancipia*, and the schalks —a conclusive evidence that not alone bondage to the soil, but positive chattelhood, prevailed in the primitive forests of Germany.

Cities and organized industry had then no existence. Freemen, *i.e.*, masters, had but a few crude wants, and these were supplied by the work of the schalks in the dwelling or in the *hof* (court) of the master. In primitive prehistoric times, as in the time of Tacitus and afterward, all the male and female household menials, peasants and workmen, were *schalks*.

Manumissions were common, but depended wholly on the will of the master. They could be obtained in various ways-might be bought with labor, produce, money, etc. The manumitted did not, however, enter at once into full enjoyment of the rights of freeman or master; indeed, only his descendants of the third generation became fully purified and capable of entering into the noble class. They then constituted, probably, the inferior nobility or freemen, who were followers and companions of the first class; and perhaps from them sprang the free yeomanry, who originally possessed but small property and a small number of schalks and serfs.

The fighting-men, or warriors, who subdued and enslaved other tribes, or transformed into schalks the weaker members of their own tribe, frequently located some of them on lands or homesteads which they permitted them to cultivate for their own use, on condition of paying a rent, generally in kind, and performing various other acts of servitude. Such was the origin of the German *liti*, who afterward constituted the common people.

The free, that is originally the *strong*, the *subduer*, was at the summit of the whole German social structure. He was free because he was absolute master over the weak, who had no power or strength in himself or family, and therefore was rightless. The genuine meaning of the word *frow* (from which is derived *fri, free, freedom,*) is "the right to own" land, *liti* and *schalks*. From *frow* comes the *frowen* "freemen," "rulers," "masters," —the caste for which all others existed. Land and schalks constituted the wealth of *frowen* or nobleman, and to acquire them the German tribes exerted all their warlike energies. All the remote Teutonic invasions, as well as those of the mediæval times, were made principally for the acquisition of land and slaves. The lands, conquered by the swords of the *frowen*, were worked by the *schalks*.

The slave traffic existed and was highly developed among the primitive Germans. It was carried on at the time of Tacitus, and some investigators maintain that for long centuries it was the only traffic known among the barbarous Germans; and slavery in its worst form was in full blast in Germany when her tribes dashed themselves against the Western empire. The slaves constituted more than half of the whole Germanic population. Wirth, the most conscientious investigator of the primitive social condition of the Germanic race, estimates the proportion of freemen to slaves as one to twenty-four. All of them —*frowen*, *adelings*, nobles of all degrees, followers, vassals, *liti* and *schalks*, lived the same simple, agrestic life. Rude in mind and of vigorous bodies, in comparatively small numbers they shattered in pieces the rotting Roman empire.

First the incursions, then the definite invasions and conquests-Attila's forays from one end of Europe to the other-gave a vigorous impulse to slavery, both abroad and at home. Abroad, the invaders enslaved all that they reached-destroying, burning, devastating, impoverishing the population, and increasing the number of those forced to seek in chattelhood a remedy against starvation. At home, immense tracts of land were depopulated and abandoned, and old and new *frowen*, masters, seized upon them. Of course *schalks* were in demand, and were supplied by traffic and kidnapping.

The wars among the Germanic tribes, which were continued more or less vigorously, and the wars with neighboring populations, increased the number of slaves thrown upon the market.

The transition of a great part of Europe from the Roman to what may be called the German world, was so terrible that for several centuries the most unparalleled destruction, desolation, and slavery constituted the principal characteristics of the first mediæval epoch.

But Europe, the Christian world, and humanity were not to be submerged in the foul mire of chattelism. The awful crisis lasted through many generations, and bloodshed and superhuman suffering were their lot. But finally, the turning-point of the disease was reached: the disorder began to yield. Often after such a crisis the malignant symptoms do not abate at once, nay, they sometimes reappear with renewed force, and a long period is needed for a complete recovery. So in the evolution of Europe, overflowed by the German tribes, the most malignant symptoms of chattelhood continued and reappeared for a long time in their worst characteristics, before the social body entered the stage of convalescence.

The bloody throes of the German world redounded to the benefit of the nobles abroad and at home. *Liti* and schalks increased, and land rapidly accumulated in the hands of the few during the first centuries of the German Christian era. Thus Saxony belonged to twenty, some say to twelve nobles, who kept thereon half-free vassals, *liti*, and schalks.

As the oligarchs of Greece and Rome and Gaul, so the German *frowen*, the powerful, the rich, in all possible ways, *per fas et nefas*, seized upon the homesteads of the poor; and the impoverished freemen or *ahrimen*, smaller nobles, and vassals, became *liti* and schalks. Analogous conditions produce analogous results in usages as in institutions and laws; and often that which appears to have been borrowed by one nation or people from another, is only a domestic outgrowth germinating from similar circumstances.

When the German lay and clerical founders of the feudal system possessed more land than they could cultivate, and when the iron hand of Charlemagne prevented domestic feuds and the supply of slaves from that source, then they kidnapped right and left, heathen and Christian, poor freeman or schalk. Some of the feudal barons of the time of Charlemagne owned as many as twenty thousand *liti* and schalks.

Karl, Karle (the correct name), or Charlemagne (the more common one), in one of his numerous edicts or capitularies, prescribes as follows to those who received lands, baronies, abbeys, etc., as fiefs or grants: "Et qui nostrum habet beneficium diligentissime prevideat quantum potest

Deo donante, ut nullus ex mancipiis (chattels) ad illum pertinentes beneficium fame moriatur, quod superest ultra illius familiæ necessitatem, hoc libere rendat jure prescripto."

Manumissions were promoted, in various ways, by the civil and clerical authorities. Many free yeomen were created from manumitted slaves, as well as from poor vassals or followers. But such were soon impoverished by wars and devastations, and were, from various causes, reduced to the condition of *liti* and chattels.

Serfdom and slavery were generally more severe in the northern portion of Germany, as Saxony, etc., than in the southern; but in both, the peasantry were crushed, oppressed, and, when it was feasible, enslaved. When Lothair I., grandson of Charlemagne, revolted against his father, Louis the Pious, he appealed for help to the oppressed peasantry, tenants, and chattels.

The centuries of the *faustrecht* —"right of the fist," that is of the sword, of brute force-soon succeeding all over Germany to Charlemagne's orderly rule, the strongholds of dynasts, barons, nobles and robbers, shot out everywhere like mushrooms; and from them radiated oppressions and exactions of every kind. The ancient practice of ruining the poor freemen and tenants, then transforming them into serfs, and then the serfs into chattels, went on as of old. In proportion as the forests were cleared, however, the baron found he could not profitably work the extensive estates with schalks alone, and that it would be more economical to transform these chattels into serfs, tenants, etc., and establish them on small parcels of his property. This was the first feeble sign of amelioration. Villages formed in this way by dynasts, or princes, and by barons, then received some rudiments of communal, rural organization.

A more powerful engine of emancipation, however, were the cities. In the course of the tenth century, dynasts, princes and emperors began everywhere to found cities, endowing them with various franchises and privileges. The legitimate flow of events, the necessities created by a settled organic existence which could only be supplied by the regular movements of industry and commerce, together with the influence of Gaul, and above all, of Italy, stimulated the German rulers. To the emperor Henry I., of the house of Saxony, belongs the glory of having given the first impulse to commerce, and thus the first blow to chattelhood and serfdom.

The population of the newly-founded cities consisted of inferior people of all kinds-laborers, operatives, small traders, poor freemen, and persons manumitted on condition of residing in the cities-the founders of the cities originally peopling them with their own retainers and with vagabonds of all kinds. Of course no nobles even of the lowest kind became burghers, and thus the first municipal patricians were of very inferior birth. Thus antagonism to barons and feudal nobles generally formed the very cornerstone of the cities.

Among the privileges granted to the first cities was that a serf, schalk, or, in a word, any bondman, seeking refuge in the precincts of a city, became free if not claimed within a year. This respite to the fugitive soon became a common law all over Germany, even between nobles in relation to their fugitive serfs; and the hunter of a fugitive lost caste even among the free masters —*freiherrn*. When a legal prosecution was attempted, every difficulty, legal and illegal, was thrown in the way of the claimant-the cities willingly resorting to arms for the defence of their right of refuge.

The first Crusades emancipated large numbers of persons, as the taking of the cross was the sign of liberty for serf and for slave. But in Germany as in France, the great and perma-nent influence of the Crusades on emancipation consisted in their strengthening the cities and impoverishing the nobles, and thus producing a salutary change in internal economic relations.

The wars of the Germans with their neighbors, and above all with the Slavonians, Magh-yars, etc., in the tenth and eleventh centuries, again gave vitality to the slave traffic; and war prisoners and captives, not now of their own kindred, but of foreign birth, were brought to the markets for sale.

Nevertheless, chattelhood was slowly dying out, and about the twelfth century but few traces of it remained: prisoners of war began to be ransomed or exchanged, and villeinage, with various services attached, altogether superseded domestic slavery.

The villein possessed the rights of family, of village, and partially of communal organization. But many of the galling characteristics of chattelhood were transfused into serfdom and villeinage. The nobles became, if possible, more insolent, exacting and oppressive. But the villeins and peasants began to feel their power, and to combine and act in common in the villages, and afterward in the communes.

Partial insurrections followed each other in various parts of Germany; here against one baron or master, there against another. Every insurrection, even if suppressed, nevertheless gave an impulse, though sometimes imperceptible, to amelioration and emancipation. Insurrections of the down-trodden and oppressed classes are like feverish efforts of diseased physiology to resist the disorder, to throw out the virus, and restore the normal condition in the economy of life. The whole world admires the glorious insurrection of the Swiss-German peasantry against *their* insolent masters. Then the bondmen, villeins, etc., individually or in small bodies, by the axe, by fire, and in every possible manner, protested their imprescriptible right to liberty. So also did the celebrated Münzer when the reformation dawned over Germany and Europe. He firmly believed that religious reform, to be beneficial to the poor, must go hand in hand with social ameliorations. The most notable insurrection, however, was the great uprising of the German peasantry in the sixteenth century. From the Vosgese mountains, from the Alps to the Baltic, numerous isolated forces rose in arms, each inspired by the same great idea. They had no centres, no possibility of a combination of effort, but all of them recognized the same covenant: 1. The gospel to be preached in truth, but not in the interest of their masters-nobles and clergy. 2. Not to pay any kind of tithes. 3. The interest or rent from landed property to be reduced to five per cent. 4. Forests to be communal property. 5. All waters free. 6. Game free. 7. Serfdom to be abolished. 8. Election of communal authorities by the respective communes. 9. Lands robbed from the peasantry to be restored to the original owners.

This great war of the peasants was terrible, pitiless, bloody. More than one thousand strongholds, burghs, and monasteries were destroyed; but the peasants were finally overpowered, the nobility being aided by the forces of the empire. Luther, too, thundered against the poor peasants.[17] But not in vain did they shed their blood. The oppression by the old *frowen*, strengthened by feudality, was finally broken at the roots. The imperial German diet declared to the nobles, that if they did not cease their cruelties, at the next revolt they should be abandoned to their fate.

Serfdom was not yet abolished, but was moderated in various ways. The direct and indirect influence of the Reformation on the condition of the peasantry has been already mentioned. Mild reforms were introduced in the dominions of various German sovereigns. Certain liberties were granted to rural communes, and the number of free tenants slowly but uninterruptedly increased. The conditions of villeinage on private estates began to be regulated by the respective governments; and absolute serfdom was slowly dying out. The prosperity of Germany increased proportionally with the emancipation, though but partial, of rural labor, and the freedom of the soil. On an average, those regions were most prosperous which contained the greatest number of emancipated rural communities, or where the villeinage was reduced, systematized, and made more and more free from the arbitrary exactions of the master.

The peculiar political organization of Germany prevented any unity of action in the extinction of rural servitude. Many of its features-some relating to the person, but principally to the soil-survived even to the present century in certain parts of the smaller German states; and in Austria, Bohemia and Hungary, there is still room for infinite improvement in the condition of the peasantry. But the mortal disorder exists no more. the fundamental rights of man are recognized. Governmental maladministration, injustice, oppressive taxation, exactions by officials and landlords, are unhappily common; but all these are in flagrant violation of established laws. And, bad though they are, they cannot for a moment compare with the blighting influences of chattel slavery.

For long centuries, and with persistent pertinacity, have slavery and the oppression of man and his labor gnawed at the German vitals; and centuries must elapse before the recovery of a normal condition. But the Germans of the present day-moralists, statesmen, savants and professional men, as well as artisans, mechanics and agriculturists-are unanimous in condemning human bondage, whatever may be the race enslaved. Few, indeed, are there of the great German race whose minds are inaccessible to the nobler promptings of freedom and humanity.

XVII. Longobards-Italians

AUTHORITIES:

Leges Longobardorum, Cantu, Troya, Karl Hegel, etc.

The Western Roman empire was fatally permeated throughout with chattel slavery. Domestic usage had made its German invaders also familiar with the art and practice of enslaving: their conquest of Rome accordingly but added strength and extension to the slave-edifice. For a longer or shorter period, various German tribes ravaged Italy. The domination of the Ostrogoths lasted for about sixty years, and the rule of Theodoric the Great is recorded as among the best and wisest in that period of devastation and oppression. Finally, the Longobards founded in Italy a permanent establishment. At the first onset, the Longobards reduced all, in city and country, to bondage: the magnate, the rich, the slaveholder, as well as the workman, the poor, the serf and the chattel, constituted their booty, and as such were divided among the victors.

Some historians maintain that all free Romans,[18] rich and poor —a few favored aristocratic families excepted-were deprived of the rights of personal liberty and property by the Longobards; others, however, assert that the free population was only made tributary, but otherwise preserved their property, rights and laws. The conquerors (as *hospites*, or quartered soldiers) generally took about a half of the houses, lands and chattels of the conquered, and furthermore compelled the primitive owner to pay them a tribute from what was left. In Italy, the Longobards made the free Romans, rich and poor, tributary to the extent of one-third of all which was left them from actual confiscation; and Paul Diaconus-himself a Longobard-says: "*Romani tributarii efficiuntur.*" The artisans and traders, and indeed all inhabitants of cities, likewise paid tribute. They could not move from one place to another without the written permission of their Longobard master; and in this way originated the system of passports for bondmen, which is still maintained in our Slave States. Thus the Romans, once proud and free, became but half free —a something between the positive freeman, such as the Longobard alone was, and the still more reduced tributaries, the *aldu* or *aldions*, and the serfs. In brief, the freemen, rich or poor, were made inferior in rights and in personal liberty to the soldiers; the non-free, the ancient *colons*, etc., were pressed a degree lower in servitude; and the condition of the domestic chattels alone remained unchanged.

The Longobards, like all the other German warriors, disliked the cities, and the chiefs and nobles erected their fastnesses outside of them. The common soldiers receiving lands in different quantities, formed the freeholders, yeomen, or *ahrimans*, and were bound to perform military duty. Such was the origin of the feudal system, which sprang up on the ruins of the Roman empire. The numerous cities of Italy had no longer any political rights or signification, though they still preserved some remains of former culture and civilization, and even faint shadows of the former municipal regime. The imperial city itself was not overrun by the Longobards, and from thence, as also from the other cities of that part of Italy which belonged to the Eastern emperors, some faint glimmerings reached the Longobard region and tended to preserve ancient municipal traditions.

The influence of the Italian polity and culture at length began to humanize the Longobards. Some of their laws concerning chattels and slaves are more humane than were those under the emperors-more humane than those now existing in our Slave States. For example, a master committing adultery with the wife of his chattel lost the ownership of both her and her husband, and had no further power over them. Various regulations also protected the serf and chattel against a cruel master, and punishment was not arbitrary, but was in many cases regulated by law. Emancipations were encouraged and protected: King Astolf's edict even proclaimed that it was meritorious to change a chattel into a freeman. However, during the first period of their dominion, the Longobards, like all the other German conquerors, in Spain, Gaul, etc., and, above all, the feudal dukes and nobles, considered the blood of the conquered as impure, and therefore far inferior to their own.

Industry and commerce gradually began to acquire vitality, and the chattels began slowly to disappear from the cities, either by emancipation, by purchasing their liberty, or by being established as *aldii* or serfs on their masters' lands.

The slave-trade was now confined principally to non-baptized prisoners-whom the Christians of that epoch regarded as the progeny of the evil one. Mahomedans, heathen, Germans, as the Anglo-Saxons and others, from various nations and tribes, were more numerous in the slave marts than were those born on the soil of Italy.

Under the Longobards, Italy again began to be more commonly cultivated by numerous *colons* with very limited rights, but still in better condition than those of the preceding epoch; copyholders and freeholders also began to increase, as has been already mentioned. So that when the heavy clouds of the mediæval times began to break, the condition of Italy was slightly improving; and when Karl, or Charlemagne, put an end to the dominion of the Longobards, more land was under culture, and the free though tributary population was greater, both in the cities and the country, than on their first invasion.

The rule of the Franks, which succeeded that of the Longobards, did not impair the condition of the Italians. Peace was beneficial to labor, labor stimulated emancipation. Thus the number of *chattels* was more and more reduced, while the serfs, *adscripti glebæ*, increased. But the disorders which succeeded the dismembering of the empire of Charlemagne again ruined many free yeomen, ahrimans, and others owning small homesteads, and obliged them to submit to the oppression of the mighty nobles. Many of the dispossessed and impoverished, however, sought refuge in the cities, where industry flourished in proportion with the freedom of the workmen and operatives. Finally, about the eleventh century, the *cities* began to strike for their independence. This was the time of the revival of the communal franchises in other parts of Europe also; but the first spark was struck in Italy. Around the standard raised by the cities crowded the serfs, rural and domestic chattels, and all other kinds of bondmen and oppressed. This was, in fact, the insurrection of these against the landed barons, nobles, and oligarchs. All runaways found refuge and protection in the cities; and hence arose the energy, the strength, and the democratic rancor of the cities against the nobility and their strongholds.

In the second part of the mediæval epoch, throughout Italy and Western Europe, prisoners of war were no more sold as slaves, but were ransomed or exchanged. The Moors and Arabs (Mahomedans) were the sole marketable chattels.

All the Italian cities extended their dominion, acquired lands, incorporated baronies, and regulated the relations between the owners of the soil and the tenants. Domestic slavery was altogether extinct; the cities were animated by free labor in their arts, industries and handicrafts, and on the estates, the peasants, serfs and bondmen, *adscripti glebæ*, became vassals obliged to follow the barons or the cities into war; they became free tenants-first paying rent for their land in kind, and then paying in money; and the number of freeholders, and others holding homesteads, continually increased. Hunting for absconded serfs now had an end. The cities and boroughs emancipated all the villagers and serfs around them. In the course of the twelfth century, personally degrading servitude of every kind almost wholly disappeared; and the relations between the proprietor of land and the farmer were established on the basis which, with more or less modification, prevails to the present day.

In the ancient classical world, in Greece and Rome, domestic slavery had its seat in the cities, and therefrom expanded over the land, destroying the whole social structure. But now, the first shout for liberty came from the Italian cities; the cities first emancipated the laborers within their own walls, and then emancipated the rural serf. Cities again became the centres of civilization; they nursed its infancy, tended its first footsteps and gave it the free air of heaven: they trained it not amid clanking chains and groaning chattels.

Thus does history annihilate the ignorant fallacy about Saxons and Germans being the godfathers of social or political freedom.

Many evils and disorders undoubtedly remained and even yet remain; but the sum of all evils-property in man and in his toil-was utterly destroyed. Then came the brilliant epoch of the Italian Lombard cities-the culminating glory of Italian civilization-whose coruscating warmth set free the whole of Western Europe.

XVIII. Franks-French

AUTHORITIES:

Augustin Thierry, Henry Martin, Bonnemère, etc.

Domestic slavery, aggravated by the oppression of the poor, the devastations of war, the insatiable necessities of the imperial treasury, the confiscations of property during the reigns of bad emperors, and other causes, ate into the very vitals of Roman Gaul. It has been already shown how the ancient relations of clansman and client merged successively into tributary *colons*, into *adscripti glebæ*, and into chattels. At the period of the final assault of the northern races on the Roman empire, in Gaul, as everywhere else, there was no people behind the imperial legions except rich slaveholders and poor degraded freemen, serfs and chattels; and the legions, too, were mostly recruited from among vagabonds and barbarians. Long before this time, Stilicon, in order to raise soldiers for his army, proclaimed freedom to the chattels who should join his standard; and by this means collected over thirty thousand men!

During the integrity of the empire, branches of the tribe of Franks dwelt in parts of northern Gaul, either as colonists, or as allies who recognized in the Roman emperor their lord paramount. From here they dealt their conquering blows; they subdued to their rule the other German races already established in Gaul, and laid the foundation of the future Carlovingian empire, and finally of France.

The Franks permitted the conquered peoples to retain their own law, which was the Roman, for all civil suits between Roman and Roman. This benefited only the freemen-of whom there were but few-and the rich, so that they could oppress the poor and treat them as they did under the empire; for the Franks did not interfere in any of their internal relations, legal or illegal. The rich and cunning Roman magnates ingratiated themselves with their conquerors: they became *antrustiones* or commensals of the kings, thus acquiring a high social and political status and influence; and there were many of them among the powerful and influential aristocracy which sprang up under the Merovingians. All the conquered paid oppressive tribute; and the rich, as of old, used every means to increase their estates, serfs and chattels from the booty and exactions made by the Franks.

But although the rights of the free Romans were thus recognized in principle, their persons and property were by no means regarded as sacred. The Franks divided the conquered lands among them in lots, and often seized, along with the estate, the whole of the personal property of a rich Roman magnate.

The Merovingians were almost continually at war among themselves, and these wars were most ruinous to the cities and the rich free Romans. When a peace was concluded, these Romans constituted the hostages for both belligerent parties; and when a peace was broken, the hostages on both sides were treated as prisoners of war; they became chattels, and their property was confiscated.

The Roman cities became the property of the kings and chiefs, the lands the property of the Frankish soldiery. The Franks also were perpetually at war either among themselves or with their neighbors. Military duty was a condition of the possession of land, so that Roman and other slaves and bondmen cultivated the soil and worked for their conquerors. During the imperial epoch, the opulent Gallic magnates and senators lived in magnificent villas, like the Roman nabobs and oligarchs in Italy, Spain, Africa, etc. During the early period of the invasions, an owner would often fortify his villa and defend it with his armed household and chattels. Such villas, changing masters, afterward, in many instances, became feudal strongholds, around each of which grew a village, which in the course of time became a borough, then a town, and finally a city. In this way the Gallo-Roman villas gave rise to the French name *village* and *ville*.

In general, with the new Frankish conquest, oppression became increasedly grievous, while the slave traffic, especially in prisoners of war, received a new impulse. In the first storm the

Roman fiscality for a moment disappeared; but it was soon restored, and with it almost the whole of the Roman administration. The Franks revolted against taxation when one of the kings tried to apply it to them, but the Roman populations bore its whole brunt. Tribute, taxes and other exactions finally became so oppressive that the poor and impoverished sold their children and sometimes even themselves into slavery. The Jews were the common mediators and factors in this traffic, as well as the most extensive slave-traders all over Europe, both then and in subsequent times; and a considerable part of the hereditary hatred of the European masses toward the Jews is to be ascribed to this historic fact.

The Frankish kings and their Frankish subjects had large estates, *métairies*, worked by serfs and chattels. The conquerors hated the cities, preferring the favorite old German life in the country, where they spent their time surrounded by their followers. The lordly mansions, the *sala* of the kings and the powerful, were erected amidst great forests in the style of encampments; and to this day the German word *hoflager*, "court-camp," is the name for the residence or court of a sovereign. Political power and prestige were no longer derived from municipal citizenship, but from the possession of land; and thus originated the feudal importance of the country and the barons, in contradistinction to the now powerless *municipium*. In the Greek and Roman world, the country was wholly sacrificed, politically and socially, to the city, which, in turn, acquired more and more political power and importance in proportion as domestic slavery destroyed the primitive yeomanry. In the early stages of feudalism scarcely any attention was paid to the cities; they are principally mentioned as sources whence taxes and tributes may be largely squeezed.

In the Free States of the American Union, also, in the townships and villages, the significance of the country has reached its highest and noblest development. Here the free townships and villages are the fountains of healthy political life, and the genuine source of all civilizing agencies.

Under the Merovingians and Carlovingians, the frequent wars and oppressions proved destructive not only to the natives but also to the conquerors themselves. The Franks and other German landholders, by their violent and disorderly mode of life, were soon impoverished and became the prey of powerful neighbors of their own kindred. The savage rigor of the law regulating composition for crimes quickly drained and utterly destroyed the patrimonies of the reckless soldiery, and thus rapidly increased the number of landless vagabonds, who were neither tenants nor serfs, but became chattels to men of their own race, once their companions and perhaps even their followers. At the end of the second Salic dynasty very few free laborers existed, and kidnapping, especially on the sea-coasts, became common.

Charlemagne, as previously mentioned, tried to regulate and alleviate the condition of the bondmen and chattels. His capitularies forbade the selling of chattels beyond the kingdom; and whoever violated this law became a slave himself. Slaves were to be sold in the presence of the count or the bishop, or their lieutenants, or notables, but not surreptitiously, or from one person to another, without being controlled by the authorities; and heavy fines also followed all violations of this law. Notwithstanding all this, however, Norman and Saracen wars and invasions, together with Frankish taxations and exactions, kept the country in the same state of desolation as during the centuries of the agonizing empire. Scarcely any towns existed, and the few large cities were scattered at enormous distances one from the other. Fastnesses, castles, burghs and fortified monasteries dotted the land; even they, however, being separated from each other by great forests and marshes. The poor and oppressed serfs and chattels were hunted and kidnapped, and no place of refuge existed for them.

Under Charlemagne, public order and protection to the free tenants, serfs and chattels, existed to as high a degree as was possible at that epoch; but with his death all this disappeared. The crisis which then occurred and which ended in consolidating the feudal social structure, was even more terrible than the epoch of invasions. The poor classes and the serfs and chattels, as we might suppose, suffered most. The tenth century marks the triumph of the feudal *régime*, and with this triumph chattelhood (*mancipium*) disappears from the laws and the usage of the oppressive masters. The chattels now became hereditary bondmen or serfs, and were no longer objects of sale or of traffic. They could not be separated from their families, but were established in villages; and the slave traffic was carried on solely in Saracens and other heathen.

In all other respects serfdom preserved almost all the most revolting features of ancient domestic slavery. The feudal lord employed the serfs as tillers of his soil, and the harvests they raised were the chief sources of his income; while they likewise formed his followers in his feuds with feudal neighbors or with his lords paramount-the counts, dukes, and kings. The feudal lord did not sell his serfs-as the churches, synods, and councils all united in condemning the traffic in Christians.

The present serf, tiller, and laborer, all over Western Europe, was the younger, outlawed member of the human family, and so now are our Southern chattels.

For a long time the difference between serfdom and ancient chattelhood was discernible only with great difficulty. The collar worn by chattels since the time of Augustus remained on the necks of the serfs (and these, too, not *adscripti glebæ*), with the expression —"I BELONG," or with the name of the master cut thereon. This was the custom in England with the Anglo-Saxon serfs of the Athelstanes and the Cedrics, so that the ancestry of the haughty Anglo-Saxon slaveholding American barons of the present day wore collars!

The feudal order was firmly established. Below the social hierarchy, composed of free fiefs, and estates belonging to nobles, churches, and monasteries (all of them free from taxation and public servitude), descend another social grade, whose only badges were humiliations, sufferings, toils, and martyrdom. Servitude and serfdom had similar gradations among the peasantry and workmen bound to the soil of their feudal master as existed among the barons, nobles, abbots, etc., in *their* various relations and duties of vassalage.

A few towns and boroughs began to spring up from the same social soil whence arose those of Germany. But the immense majority of the nobles and owners of cities considered their inhabitants, at the best, as but half free, as tributaries or *censitaires*, and continually attempted to plunge them deeper into servitude and villeinage. The remnants of the independent yeomanry, free tenantry, copyholders, etc., rapidly disappeared. These descendants of the conquerors-of kindred race, too, with the barons-accepted servitude in order to find patronage and alleviation from further oppression, or else sought refuge in the cities and towns, abandoning their homesteads, which were seized by the feudal baron and annexed to his estate.

All along the twelve or fifteen centuries which extend from the decline of the Greek and Roman republics and the first days of the empire down to the consolidation of feudalism, it is evident that similar causes were ever in operation, depriving the poor of their property, their labor, and finally of their liberty —a result, too, brought about in every case in an identical manner. In this, as in many other things, the history of the human race and its disorders and woes is a record of almost continuous analogies.

The smaller feudal masters, afterward called *hoberaux*, were generally the most cruel and inhuman then, as well as afterward, during the long protracted centuries of serfdom of the French peasantry. Tyranny always becomes fiercer and more maddened in proportion as the circle of its power and action is diminished. Is it not so also on American slave plantations?

It has been already mentioned, that the kings and the more powerful feudal vassals began to erect towns, and that these towns served as refuges for the homeless, and also for the serfs. The lesser nobles and the feudalized clergy often upbraided the kings for thus depopulating their estates; while the barons who owned the cities soon exasperated their inhabitants by their exactions and cruelties.

Such were the prominent domestic and economic features of the times of feudalism and chivalry in France, as over the whole of Europe. It is for other reasons that, in the minds of some, a halo still surrounds their memory and their name. But, penetrating behind that halo, what a horrid spectacle of tyranny, oppression, and cruelty meets the eye! The sham chivalry of our Slave States has not even the shadow of such an aureola to hide its hideousness. The cruel and reckless barons sprang from a reckless race, in an age of darkness: they had no other traditions from the past, no other example before them. But the American chivalry and knight-errants of slavery spit on all the noble traditions transmitted by their sires. They have before their eyes the spectacle of freedom generating prosperity in all ages. And yet with all this do they deliberately turn their backs upon the light, and rush heedlessly toward dark barbarity.

The feudal rights of the barons in the products and earnings of the tradesmen and workmen, as well as in the person and labor of the serfs, together with their right of civil and criminal jurisdiction, were all the result of successive usurpations.

Toward the end of the eleventh, and especially in the twelfth century, the cities and towns rose against their feudal oppressors. This great movement was not preconcerted, nor was it instigated by outside conspirators. The cities, goaded by exactions and oppressions, rose separately, and each one on its own account. The impulse came from man's natural aspirations for freedom and justice, and his hatred of tyranny. The true conspirators were the nobles who oppressed the cities. Louis VI., of immortal memory, aided the cities in their efforts to form themselves into communes, gave them charters, and relieved them from the power of the barons; in short, he did every thing possible to undermine the power of the nobles, and prevent them from pillaging, torturing, and murdering the people. But the emancipation of the cities was finally achieved only by blood; and the kings, moved by humanity as well as policy, supported the citizens in their efforts, and thus reduced the tyrannic and unruly barons and nobles. The nobles, small and great, in France as in other parts of Europe, resisted with arms the communal emancipation. They proclaimed and treated as rebels and subverters of order and society, all who tried to reconquer their liberty, as well as all those who advocated the cause of the oppressed. Does not the same phenomenon reappear in our own time and country?

With the emancipation of the cities and the formation of communes, civilization began to illumine the horizon of France. But this great social event had not such a direct influence on the condition of the rural populations in France as it had in Italy. Still the serfs found a safe refuge in the now independent cities.

The crusades acted in the same way on the condition of the peasantry in France, as they did in Germany, Flanders, etc.

Successively, kings began to regulate and alleviate the condition of the serfs on their domains, gradually interposing to limit the power of the nobles over their serfs. A chronicler of that time (twelfth century), says: "*Cetera censuum exactiones quæ servis infligi solent* (nobles) *omnimodis vacent.*" The French legists of the thirteenth century, inspired by Ulpian and Roman law, the study of which was again revived by a decree of Louis IX., declared that every man on the soil of France is or ought to be free, by right as well as by the law of nature. Subsequently this axiom was considered applicable even to Saracens, Mahomedans, Africans, and all races, creeds, and nationalities. Louis IX. was the friend of the oppressed and the redresser of the wrongs of the peasantry. He abolished the more oppressive servitudes in the domains, and tried to humanize the nobles.

The great principle of liberty asserted by the legists of the thirteenth century, was in the fourteenth embodied in a law or edict of Louis X., which decreed that the serfs might pay off their personal and rural obligation to the nobles and become free tenants. This law was very generally carried out in the royal domains, but did not find much favor among the nobles or in the feudalized church. At that time, moreover, many serfs and peasants, from poverty, mental degradation, and shiftlessness, and others from distrust of the law and the nobles, refused the freedom offered to them. In several provinces, disorders even resulted from their resistance, especially in those places where the conditions dictated by the seneschals (royal overseers), nobles, and priests, were so oppressive as to make free tenantry no better than bondage, and for this reason, also, serfs who had obtained their liberty often returned to servitude. In defence of American chattelhood, it is asserted that many chattels spurn the idea of emancipation; that many of them, when emancipated, return, of their own choice, into slavery, and that they are too degraded to appreciate freedom, and too shiftless to achieve its rewards. These very reasons, based on facts similar to those now set forth, were urged by the French feudal masters against the efforts of the government to liberate the oppressed whites.

The consequences of a bodily as of a social disorder are frequently of protracted duration. The oppression of centuries so destroys the mind and manhood of the oppressed that they consider slavery their normal condition, even as physical monstrosities have sometimes been regarded by their possessors as the symbols of beauty and health. Such incurables may even be found among the now free descendants of social, political, national, and legal bondmen-among the descendants of those who in former times were covered with contempt, and who suffered unutterable social degradation. Such are the Irish, *en masse*, and some others who escape oppression in Europe only to support slavery in America.

Personal serfdom and vassalage began to be gradually modified; but on the estates of the clergy and nobility it lasted till near the eighteenth century, still preserving several of its worst features. Nowhere in Europe was the peasant so long and so grievously oppressed as in France; nowhere did he take such terrible but just revenge. Insurrections of the peasantry in various parts of France form an almost uninterrupted historic series, of which the great revolution was the fitting climax.

The repeated *bagaudies* of the Gallic peasantry have been already mentioned: the next revolt was in the tenth century, when the serfs and peasants of Neustræ (Normandy) rose against the Northmen, who had just established themselves, and who tried to transform them into chattels; and another rising took place about the same time in Brittany. Beside many partial uprisings against particular strongholds or districts, the most general and most celebrated were those of the *pastouraux*, in the thirteenth and fourteenth centuries-one of which was directed principally against the feudalized clergy-and the repeated *jacqueries*. Indeed, during the fourteenth century, the whole of Europe might be said to be divided into two great hostile camps: the nobles with their exactions and oppressions forming one, and the laborers, peasants and serfs, resisting their oppressors with battle-axe and fire, forming the other. And thus the oppressed everywhere hewed out their path to freedom and civilization.

The fifteenth, sixteenth and seventeenth centuries had their various revolts, sometimes evoked by governmental measures and maladministration, but far oftener stirred up by the reckless and cruel treatment of the laborer by the nobles-against whom both the law and royal authority were too often inefficient and powerless.

Then came the epoch of atonement and of justice —1789-1793. Then germinated the seeds which had been sown for centuries in the social soil by the oppressors, and then, too, was gathered the bloody harvest.

The present rural population or peasantry of France, the descendants of serfs and chattels, now possess the same civil and political rights as any other class in the nation-rights more ample than are enjoyed by any other peasantry in Europe. They have, of course, still to suffer various evils arising from the common imperfection of all social structures; but no special degradation is attached to their birth or their condition.

The first glimpses of mental culture, in the earliest mediæval night, came from the monasteries-from monks who generally belonged to the conquered race, or sprang from chattels and serfs. Indeed, almost all the modern European civilization was elaborated in the cities by the so-called middle classes, and by peasants. Luther and Kepler were the sons of poor peasants; and the sires of the immense majority of the European middle classes, at one time or another, were chattels, serfs, or bondmen, who were for ages considered and treated as brutes by the nobles and barons. All over Europe many of the genealogies of aristocratic families ascend to slaves, serfs and villeins.

XIX. Britons, Anglo-Saxons, English.

AUTHORITIES:

Domesday-book, Sharon Turner, Lappenberg, Pauli, Hallam, Brougham, Vaughan, etc.

The social condition of the Britons previous to the invasion of Cæsar was in all probability similar to that of their kindred Gauls. They lived in clans; the soil was held by a tenure similar to that which prevailed among the Gauls, and was tilled by clansmen or free laborers. Slavery was then, if possible, even more insignificant among the Britons than among the Gauls; and the slaves consisted of criminals and prisoners of war, and were the common property of the clan. The laboring classes were not impoverished, nor were they dependent upon the chiefs as in Gaul at the time of the Roman conquest. For various reasons Rome's influence did not operate so fatally on the Britons as it did on the Gauls; neither the culture of Rome nor her disorganizing and oppressive administration permeated Britain to the same extent as they did the rest of the empire. Still Roman rule seems to have altered somewhat the primitive relations between the chiefs and their clansmen, impoverishing the latter and corrupting the former. The Roman rule was propitious to slavery; it surrounded the powerful natives with dependents and chattels, while the poor gradually lost their freedom, and began to cultivate the soil less for their own sake than on account of their chiefs. The dissolution of former social relations was effected and the impoverishment of the people fearfully increased, by the uninterrupted invasions of the Picts and Scots, and by the Anglo-Saxon conquest.

The Anglo-Saxons, spreading over the land, enslaved its former owners, selling them abroad or making them work for the conquerors at home. The Anglo-Saxons planted on the soil of Britain their German mode of life and their social organism in all its details. They brought with them their bondmen and slaves, their laws and usages relating to slavery, to the possession of the soil, and to composition for crime (all of which have been explained in former pages). Under the Anglo-Saxons and Danes, the chattels consisted of the descendants of the slaves existing in Roman times, as well as natives newly enslaved, criminals, debtors and captives taken in war. The Anglo-Saxon families also had slaves of Scotch and Welsh birth, generally from the borders; while, on the other hand, many Anglo-Saxons were kept in bondage by the Scotch and Welsh. Turner says: "It is well known that a large proportion of the Anglo-Saxon population was in a state of slavery; they were conveyed promiscuously with the cattle."

The Anglo-Saxon slaves were called *theow esne* and *wite-theows*, or penal slaves. Their condition was attended with all the horrors of slavery. They were kept in chains, were whipped, branded, and wore collars. They were sold in the markets, especially in London, and were at times exported beyond the sea, and found their way even to the markets of Italy and Rome. Every one knows that it was the exposition for sale of Anglo-Saxon slaves in the Roman market which resulted in the introduction of Christianity into Britain. Christianity softened the savage customs of the Anglo-Saxons, and greatly promoted emancipation; and this again increased the number of freemen and half-freemen, which formed the lower class of the population.

The division into classes-castes almost-was very rigidly observed by the Anglo-Saxons. The powers and rights of nobles, and of those who reached a high position as royal officials or owners of extensive landed property, were very great. The possession of land gave a higher political *status*, and conferred greater power among the Anglo-Saxons than among any of the other German tribes settled throughout Europe.

The free yeomen, or owners of land in fee simple, sought protection from the *hlaford* or mighty lord. For this they bartered away, partially, both their freedom and their right to the land-as was customary also among the German and all other ancient nations. The Anglo-Saxon yeomen were, in general, in a subordinate condition; they had no law, and their freedom consisted principally in having the right to change masters. The tradesmen also were, for the most part, in a servile state, and were manumitted like other chattels. Some of the manumitted slaves became agricultural laborers and hired land from the clergy, the great, the thanes or the *ealdormen*, paying them an annual rent in produce or money; but many of them also went into the towns and became burghers. Some of the burghers, also, were subject to barons and other lords, as the king; indeed, the burghers generally were not actual freeholders, and, if they were free, often had not wholly escaped the domestic service of their masters. The condition of the immense majority of Anglo-Saxons was therefore far from real freedom.

The Norman conquest transformed many landlords into tenants, while the humbler classes passed into the hands of the new masters. They became the tenants and laborers of the Norman, for whom otherwise the conquered land would have been worthless. But the Norman conquest rendered Saxon servitude so galling, that villeinage was nearly equal to chattelhood.

The "Domesday-book" gives 25,000 as the number of slaves in England. The great bulk of the rural population was composed of bondmen, or villeins under various designations-as *bordiers*, *geburs*, *cotsetlas*, etc. —who were compelled to pay oppressive imposts, and submit to various degrading and oppressing servitudes. These oppressions and exactions bore most heavily on the Anglo-Saxon population.

Slaves and serfs attached to the soil might be sold in the market-place, at the pleasure of their owners. Husbands sold their wives, and parents, unable or unwilling to support their children, might dispose of them in the same manner. The English slave-dealer of the eleventh and twelfth centuries, sold his Anglo-Saxon commodities to the Irish. A law enacted in 1102, prohibited this "wicked trade;" but the law was eluded, the trade continued, and when Henry II. invaded Ireland, he found English slaves there, whom he manumitted. In order to increase the revenue, as also from other motives of policy, the royal power in England, as all over Europe, generally favored the oppressed; its tendency always was to curb the arbitrary exactions of the barons, to promote emancipation, and generally to aid the serfs. William the Conqueror ordered that the lords should not deprive the husbandmen of their land; he enacted regulations to prevent arbitrary enslavement, and prohibited the sale of slaves out of the country. He also enacted a law which provided that the residence of any serf or slave for a year and a day, without being claimed, in any city, burgh, walled town or castle, should entitle him to perpetual liberty.

An independent freeholding yeomanry existed in comparatively small numbers. The recklessness of the feudal barons obliged the yeomanry, for the sake of protection, to render allegiance to the manor, and thus, about a century after the conquest, almost all the small homesteads disappeared. The conquered population held their property, not by absolute right, but by a tenure from the lord. Thus all individual freedom, except that of the nobles, became either entirely lost, or more and more contracted, till finally time and circumstance partly loosened, partly destroyed, the bonds which held the nation in slavery. In England as in the whole of Europe, feudal oppression was the growth of a very few generations; but it has required many hundreds of years to destroy it. A disease may be caught in an hour-years may be required for its cure. For the conquered race, the Norman had all the contempt common to conquerors. Macaulay says that when Henry I. married an Anglo-Saxon of princely lineage, many of the barons regarded it as a Virginia planter might regard marriage with a quadroon girl. But personal and economical interests obliged the barons to relent in their treatment of their serfs and chattels; and many of them were allowed under certain conditions to cultivate small portions of land.

The Saxon servile class, embraced under the general name of villeins, by and by began to have a permanent and legal interest in the land they cultivated, tilling it under the condition of a copyhold. The number of tenants on the manorial lands thus rapidly increased. But for a long period, even though the law declared that no man was a villein, still less a chattel, unless a master claimed him (and while to all others he was a freeman, eligible to have and hold property), still the nobles often seized and appropriated to themselves the property of the poorer class.

The laws under the Plantagenets, although in some respects hard for the villeins, indirectly favored their emancipation, and threw many obstacles in the way of suits brought to reclaim fugitives.

The influence of the cities on the condition of the serfs in England was similar to that which they exercised everywhere else in Europe. As under the Anglo-Saxons, so under the Normans, the inhabitants of the cities were originally serfs and villeins, or their descendants. The Plantagenets were unceasingly at war, and the enlistment of soldiers opened up an avenue to emancipation; and predial and feudal servitude of every kind ended forever with the performance of military service on land or sea. So also the serf or villein obtained freedom in various ways-through the law of refuge in cities, by being drafted into the royal service, and finally by the tenure of the land on which the baron may have established him at his own baronial pleasure. Thus by degrees arose the right of copyhold lands; and Edward III. prohibited the lords from appropriating such lands when service was rendered or the rent regularly paid.

Forced servitude steadily diminished, and the estate-holders complained that the cities and towns absorbed the labor necessary for agriculture. In 1345, Parliament regulated the wages for all kinds of farm-work, and made labor obligatory when paid for in money, but not as personal servitude. Gradually the economic and social relations became more and more those of employer and laborer, and less and less those of master and serf. Still the nobles and estate-holders continually evaded the laws, and preserved, as much as they possibly could, their oppressive rights. Against these the peasants protested by various petty insurrections.

Wat Tyler and his peasant-followers demanded that the existing remnants of villeinage should be abolished, and that the land-rent be payable in money and not in personal services, and also that the trades and market-places be free from vexatious tolls and imposts. But Wat Tyler fell-the insurrection was suppressed-the barons and lords compelled the king to break the promises he had made, and the "shoeless ribalds," as the nobles called the insurgent rustics, were forced back to their former condition. But in a little over a century afterward, villeinage wholly disappeared. Contumely, oppression, and even butchery proved in the long run quite powerless against the efforts of the oppressed classes to reconquer their freedom.

The wars of the roses dissolved many of the old liens, destroyed various domestic relations, and yet, with all their devastations, on the whole rather promoted the emancipation of land and labor. Richard III. made various regulations favorable to the peasantry and destructive of the still remaining vestiges of servitude. On this account, as well as for other reasons, some historians defend the memory of Richard III.; and it really seems that at first Richard was a good and upright man. But violent passions, lust of power, hatred of whoever opposed him or stood in his way, drove him step by step to measures of violence and to murder; and so he stands in history, a hideous and accursed monster in human form, reeking in the blood of his victims. Nations and parties often run the same career of violence and crime as individuals. Let the pro-slavery faction of to-day, which already begins to move in the bloody tracks of Richard, take warning!

Under the Tudors but few traces of the former villeinage are to be found; still it survived until the reigns of Mary and Elizabeth. But throughout the whole of the centuries during which rural servitude was slowly but steadily passing away, relics of a very stringent personal servitude, almost equal to slavery, lingered in the baronial manors and castles, in the personal relation between the masters and their retainers and menials. Against these remains of rural villeinage, vassalage, and slavery, the Henries and Elizabeths exercised their royal power, and issued decrees bearing on the subject generally, as well as others relating to special cases.[19]

It is not necessary to record here-what every student in history knows-that in proportion as servitude began to decay, the prosperity of England increased, and that from its final abolition in every form dates the uninterrupted growth in wealth and power of the English nation. The abolition of rural servitude gave a vigorous impulse to agriculture, and secured to it its present high social significance; and now the old nobility all over Europe are proud to be agriculturists. Agriculture is now a science, and it is by freedom that it has thus reached the highest honor in the hierarchy of knowledge and labor.

Through such various stages passed the Anglo-Saxons and the English people, in their transition from chattelhood and various forms of personal servitude, to freedom. The present inhabitants of English towns, as well as the free yeomanry and tenants-in brief, all the English commercial, trading, farming and working classes-have emerged from slavery, serfdom or servility. In the course of centuries the oppressed have achieved the liberty of their persons and labor, and the freedom of the soil: they have conquered political status and political rights; and their descendants peopled the American colonies, and here finally conquered the paramount right of national independence. The genuine freemen of the great Western Republic are not ashamed but proud of such a lineage of toil and victory. These freemen now and here again boldly and nobly enter the lists to combat with human bondage in every shape; and thus they remain true to the holy traditions which they have inherited from their fathers.

XX. Slavi, Slavonians, Slaves, Russians

AUTHORITIES:

Schaffarick, Corpus Scriptorum Historiæ Byzantinæ, Nestor, Fischer, Karamzin, Gerebtzoff, etc.

At what epoch the Slavic race left the common home of the Aryans and immigrated into Europe, will forever remain an insoluble mystery. Some ethnologists suppose the Slavi to have preceded the Gauls, and think they find their traces all over central Europe, on the Po, and around the Adriatic Gulf. At all events, the Slavi are very ancient occupants of European soil, and without doubt took possession of it long before the Germans. The region between the Danube, the Vistula and the Volga, was from time immemorial, as it still is, distinctly a Slavic region, although at some previous time, it was probably occupied by the Yellow or Finnic races. Subsequently the Slavi covered the lands between the Vistula and the Elba (now again lost), and colonized the southern shores of the Danube.

From immemorial time, the Slavi were an agricultural people; and perhaps they were the first who cultivated the virgin soil of Central and Northern Europe. The Slavi lived in villages, and were organized in rural communes, electing their chiefs, (*joupan*) or ancients (*starschina*). As early as the time of Herodotus, the commerce in grain was very active at the mouth of the Dnieper, and then, as at the present day, the Slavi imported their wheat to Byzantium (Constantinople), Greece, and Asia Minor.

The region occupied by the Slavi, from the Volga, along the Don (or Tanais) and the Danube, was the highway of the various branches of the Mongolian, Finnic, Uralian, Scythic, or Turanian family, in their invasions. All these old and classic denominations for the inhabitants of Asia, north of Baktria and the Himalayan mountains, are now merged in that of Tartars. So, in remote antiquity, Tartar Scythians, mixed with Slavi, dwelt on the Tanais, north of the Danube, and very likely on the plains east of the Dnieper. Other invasions of Asiatic Tartars, as Huns, Avars, Bulgars, Maghyars, Petschenegues, Polovtzy, Ugri, Turks and Tartars proper-doubtless early familiarized the primitive agricultural Slavi with the horrors of war, oppression and enslavement. And among the slaves which, under the name of Scythians, the Phenicians and Greeks trafficked in, there were doubtless some of Slavic origin.

It was very late when the Slavic race began to take part in the European or Western movement. Neither in the remotest times, nor in the great Western impulse during the early part of the Christian era, do the Slavi appear as invaders or conquerors on their own account. For many centuries, the Slavi in their relations with other races and nations, must rather be considered a passive or recipient than an expanding or creative race. For these reasons slavery does not seem to have been indigenous in those parts of the Slavic family which constituted independent groups, at the time when the race first dawns upon the horizon of history.

The Emperor Mauritius, in the sixth century, in giving an account of the defensive warfare of the Slavi, says that when they made prisoners in war, they kept them as such for a year, and afterward left it to their own choice either to settle among them or return to their native country. Thus, at an epoch when perpetual war raged all over the world, when from time immemorial prisoners of war everywhere formed the bulk of the slaves for domestic labor and for traffic, the Slavi alone were humane toward their captives.

The Slavi, however, became diseased by slavery, partly from external infection-partly from the internal development of events similar in character to those pointed out in other nations as the origin of slavery; and having once taken hold of the nation, it worked in a similar way as in other lands. For here again we see the ever recurring analogy between the origin, nature, and workings of social and bodily diseases-the same everywhere, under the equator as around the pole.

In the tenth and eleventh centuries, the Germans, under the Saxon emperors, carried on a war of conquest, almost of extermination, against the Slavi, from the Baltic along the Elbe to the Styrian and Carinthian Alps. The number of war-prisoners and peaceful settlers carried away and enslaved was immense. Many of them were sold in the Baltic ports, others in Venice, others again were distributed in the interior of Germany, and in such vast numbers that from them arose the general designation of "*slaves*" to all chattels of whatever race; and such was the origin of the word, which was afterward incorporated into all the languages of Europe.[20] Subsequently the harshest feudal tenures regulated the condition of the rural population of Bohemia, Moravia and Hungary, which did not terminate till the events of 1848-'49 put a final end to villeinage (*robot*) in all these countries.

The Poles and Russians were unaffected by feudalism in any of its social or constructive developments. Up to the seventh and eighth centuries, the Poles continued to elect their chiefs from all classes of the people-merchants and workmen. The prince or chief Leschko was a merchant; while Piast was a wheelwright, and became the founder of a long line of kings. But wars created the men of the sword, or nobility; and then in Poland, as everywhere else, the nobles began to encroach upon the rights and property of the weak, and to oppress the agriculturists, the free yeomen (*kmets, kmetones*), and the husbandmen (*gospodarsch*); but neither of these were ever transformed into chattels. When the Poles became a distinct historical nation, chattelhood was disappearing from Europe. Their contests were principally with other Slavic nations and with the Germans; and no traces are to be found of the enslavement of prisoners of war. Their heathen neighbors were the Prussians, the Iadzwingi, and Lithuanians; and captives made among them were used either in public labors or strictly in domestic service, as were also prisoners of war in after-times made from the Tartars and Turks. When these prisoners became Christians, their chattelhood was at an end.

The name for a war-prisoner is *niewolnik*, "one deprived of the exercise of his will." When the Polish agriculturists were subjugated by the nobles, and their condition became that of villeins, or *adscripti glebæ*, they began to be called *kholop* (a name most likely borrowed from the Russian), also *poddany*, "subject;" and the rural relations had the general name of *poddanstwo*, "subjection."

The Biblical narrative of the curse of Noah upon Ham furnished an easy justification for reducing the people to bondage. Peasant (*kholop*) and Ham became synonymous in the mouths of the nobles and the clergy, who generally sprang from the nobility. The oppression of the nobles was absolute during the domestic wars of the twelfth and thirteenth centuries. The people resisted, but after various partial but bloody struggles, the peasantry were subjected. In the royal domains the old yeomen (*kmetones*) still preserved their lands and some of their rights, and to the last days of Poland, the peasantry of the domains never became, either legally or in fact, *adscripti glebæ*. Casimir the Great, a Polish king of the middle of the fourteenth century, protected the rights of the peasantry against the oppressions of the nobles, and advised the peasants to defend themselves with flint and steel. He won the name of "king of the poor oppressed peasants" (*krol khlopkow*): perhaps it was the gratitude of the oppressed which conferred this title upon him, or perhaps it may have been a sneering epithet applied by the nobles. Goading indeed was the oppression of the nobles, and crushing in the extreme the servitude of the peasantry; but it never reached the point of chattelhood, excepting in rare cases of absolute lawlessness.

The *kmetones*, or free yeomen, and the husbandmen still generally remained in possession of the lands which were once their immediate property, but now only as possessors at the pleasure of the master-paying him a rent or tribute, in kind or labor, and deprived of the right of changing their domicile. The master could, at pleasure, elevate the tenant to a freeholder, or emancipate any of his household servants. The cities did not furnish such a sure refuge for runaways as did the cities in other parts of Europe. Military service, here as elsewhere, gave perpetual liberty to the bondman.

The Polish nobility had supreme sway, and were all in all; they constituted the nation, the legislators and the sovereign-even the kings being controlled by the nobles and their interests.

The nobles have paid dearly for their tyranny and oppression, as they themselves now admit that serfdom was the principal cause of the downfall of Poland.

After the dismemberment of Poland, Friederich Wilhelm III. restored personal liberty to the peasantry in the parts of the kingdom which were allotted to Prussia; in the Austrian portion, the condition of the peasantry was ameliorated and their personal liberty partially restored by Joseph II.; while that part of Poland which, at the end of the eighteenth century, was annexed, or rather reannexed, to Russia-as Lithuania and the Russian provinces-came under the control of the regulations prevailing in the empire. In Poland proper, all the peasantry are now free and enjoy full civil rights; and even the soil tilled by the peasants will soon be fully freed from every kind of predial servitude attached to its possession: and thus the peasantry will recover at least a part of the property taken from them by violence or subterfuge long centuries ago.

The Slavonians in what is now called Russia proper-from Lake Peypus and the Waldai Heights down to the banks of the Dnieper-lived, from time immemorial, in villages; these, again, were formed into smaller or larger districts (*obschtschestwo*, *wolost*), which elected for themselves their chiefs or heads (*golowa*).

Among the few cities in Russia, the great republican and commercial emporiums of Novgorod and Pskoff-well known and flourishing at the dawn of the mediæval epoch-formed the centres of that Slavic region. No nobility existed then, no slaves, and no bondmen. In 862 the republicans of Novgorod, distracted by domestic feuds and party dissensions, invited a Scandinavian, Nordman, or Variægue leader, called Rurick, to take upon himself the government of their republic. Rurick and his followers extended the Variægue supremacy as far as the southern region of the Dnieper, and Kieff became the capital of the Russian empire. At the commencement of this Variægue rule, no positive change was introduced into the internal organism of society, or the condition of the population. Rurick and his descendants were elected or confirmed by the Slavonic people, and he governed the cities and districts through his companions-in-arms or lieutenants. These, together with the direct descendants of Rurick, under the various designations of princes (*kniaz* and *mouja*), vassals, and warriors, were the founders of the Russian nobility. This, however, could not be called feudalism, as these functionaries corresponded somewhat with the counts and *missi dominici*, or lieutenant-deputies of Charlemagne. The grand-princes or grand-dukes of Kieff made war upon various tribes, mostly those of Mongolian or Tartar origin, and swept south of the Dnieper along the shores of the Black Sea down to the Caucasus; they repeatedly invaded the Byzantine empire, sometimes reaching even the suburbs of Constantinople. Then the war-prisoners and captives became domestic chattels, and chattels were also purchased from neighboring tribes and imported into Russia.

The name for a chattel, of whatever origin, is *rab*, *raba*, probably derived from *rabota*, "labor." Such *rabs* were employed in various kinds of labor, but principally in clearing the forests and cultivating the soil for their masters. Through contact with the Byzantine empire Christianity came into Russia, besides various other usages.

At this epoch, a new form of servitude appeared among the Russians; perhaps it was borrowed from the old society and civilization, or perhaps it originated from a new concatenation of circumstances: it was servitude by mutual agreement or *kabala*, by which one man gave up his person, labor, and liberty to another. This kind of bondman was called *kholop*. His servitude was usually contracted for a limited time, though sometimes for life; but was never inherited. Debts could be paid by the *kabala* writ.

The poor freeman could become a *kholop* by his own choice, or he could give up his children as *kholops*, as was then the custom among all nations, heathen and Christian. Such *kabala-kholop*, or servile person, could not be sold or disposed of in any way, as his servitude was limited in duration by specified time or by his death. Sometimes freemen choose servitude in order to escape worse conditions. Early in the domestic economy of the nation, free tenants are found who hired lands for a year or more, paying the rent (*obrog*) in money, or binding themselves to cultivate half of the land for the proprietor and half for themselves. A subsequent law prohibited any such free tenants from contracting any work or *kabala* servitude with the landowners. The contracts of free tenants were obligatory for a year from St. George's day (April 17); but otherwise they could change their domicile or land at pleasure. The laws of the tenth and eleventh centuries stringently prohibit the infliction of any kind of corporal punishment on such free tenants. In short, these tenants had full civil liberty and full civil rights; they could own lands, and could become members of any rural or urbane community, practice any handicraft, etc.

Probably it was the nobles, the rich, the higher officials, who first established chattels (*rabs*) on their lands as tillers. From these originated, beside the *rab*, the *krepostnoi kholop*, "a serf strengthened or chained to his master," *krepok* signifying "strong," "strengthened," "attached by force" —*krepost*, "stronghold," etc. According to the laws collected or enacted by Vladimir and Yaroslaw in the tenth and eleventh centuries, *rab* and *krepostnoi kholop* were the descendants of prisoners of war, or of those who were bought as slaves and imported as such into Russia, and also the descendants of those who unconditionally married a slave woman; while the public, grand-ducal slaves or *rabs* were condemned criminals.

Free tenants on the lands of the nobles, individual freeholders (*odnodwortsy*), etc., and the numerous rural communities owning land unconditionally and paying therefrom tribute-rather as public taxation-to the ducal treasury, constituted the rural population of Russia. From the time of Yaroslaw to the end of the sixteenth century, not one-tenth of the population was in the condition of *rab*, *krepostnoi kholop*, or serfs by writ or *kabala*.

The almost boundless extent of land constituting Russia was as yet unsurveyed, and no regular limits divided or marked the landed property. Thus it was easy for the strong to encroach on the lands of the rural communes, or on the new clearings made by individual freemen; and such annexations were often practised during the domestic wars between the numerous dukes, and during the time of Tartar domination. Iwan the Great (1462-1503) ordered, that whoever held a piece of land in undisputed possession for three years became its legal owner. But even the encroachments of the nobles did not transform the free laborers or tenants into serfs; and when a landlord was oppressive, whole villages abandoned him and contracted for land on other estates.

Chattels (*rab*, *krepostnoi kholop*) might be emancipated by the free will of the master; and a captive carried away by the Tartars, or a prisoner of war if a *kholop*, became free if he succeeded in escaping from captivity and returning to his country.

In the sixteenth century, all classes of the rural population began to be called Christians (*krestianin*), the Tartars having bestowed this denomination on them; and this name is now legally in use. Under Tartar dominion the rural communities paid tribute per head; and for this reason their members could not change their domicile without giving security to the commune. But after the overthrow of the Tartars by Iwan the Great, they recovered the freedom of circulation.

The primitive grand-dukes of Kief granted appanages to their younger children, and sometimes a free rural commune constituted such an appanage. Vladimir, and after him Yaroslaw, divided the empire among their children; and thus originated the rather independent dukedoms of Twer, Smolensk, Wiazma, etc. The number of appanaged princes increased; and when, after a long and bloody struggle, the grand-dukes of Moscow *mediatized* all these small dukes, appanages became private property, and the rural communes were owned by the dukes (*kniazia*), but under similar conditions of freedom as the communes constituting the public domains.

Toward the end of the sixteenth century, Borys Goudenoff-an ambitious, unscrupulous, but highly-gifted *parvenu* —got control of the weak-minded Tsar Feodor, ruled during his lifetime, became regent of the empire after his death, and finally a murderer and usurper. To ingratiate himself with the nobility and the Bojars, in 1593 he published an edict (*oukase*), by which the free tenants were henceforth prohibited from changing their masters or their domicile, and were at once reduced to serfs, *adscripti glebæ*. This first oppression quickly generated others still more odious, which stopped not till they ended in all the turpitude of chattelhood —thus justifying the saying of Lessing: "Let the devil but get hold of one single hair, and he soon clutches you by the whole queue." So in 1597 a very rigorous oukase was published concerning the restitution of fugitive serfs, their wives, children and movables. Another oukase, ordering a census of all domestic servants to be taken, transformed into serfs even those who, six months before, had entered private service as absolute freemen. With the exception of the population in the free communes constituting the tsarian domains, all the other rural populations were thus transformed into serfs in the brief space of a few years.

During the seventeenth century, the tsars of the house of Romanoff confirmed these oukases. However, the serfs were not included in the sale of an estate, neither was it permitted to transfer them from one estate to another. There were various specific denominations for the different forms of servitude, according to the nature of the labor, the quantity of produce, or the number of days' service levied by the master.

In 1718, Peter the Great ordered a general census to be taken all over the empire. The census officials, most probably through thoughtlessness or caprice, divided the whole rural population into two sections: 1st. The free peasants belonging to the crown or its domains; and 2dly. All the rest of the peasantry, the *krestianins* or serfs living on private estates, were inscribed as *khrepostnoie kholopy*, that is, as chattels. The primitive Slavic communal organization thus survived only on the royal domain, and there it exists till the present day. The census of Peter having thus fairly inaugurated chattelhood, it immediately began to develop itself in all its turpitude. The masters grew more reckless and cruel; they sold chattels separately from the lands; they brought them singly into market, disregarding all family ties and social bonds. Estates were no more valued according to the area of land they contained, but according to the number of their chattels, who were now called souls (*duschy*). In short, all the worst features of chattelism, as it exists at the present day in the American Slave States, immediately followed the publication of this accursed census.

The rural communes upon the royal domains, however, still preserved their ancient organization and even comparative freedom; but Peter the Great, as well as all his successors, rewarded his favorites, or those rendering public service, with estates or grants of land; and as such grants were taken from the royal domains, in this way hundreds of thousands of free peasants were transformed into chattels. Catharine II. also distributed great numbers of such estates among her favorites, besides confirming all the privileges of the nobility; and so likewise did Paul I. Alexander I. desired to exempt the peasants in this transfer; but Nicholas I. in reality was the first emperor who granted estates excepting therefrom the resident peasantry; he also published an oukase that henceforth no rural communes from the domains shall be granted to private individuals. Paul I., in 1797, reduced the weekly servitude of the kholop to three days, the other three remaining to himself.

Alexander I. desired to emancipate the serfs throughout the whole empire, but only succeeded, and that very partially, in the so-called German or Baltic provinces-where, moreover, the German nobles and landowners succeed in impoverishing the peasants even more after emancipation than they could before. Alexander I. also prohibited the sale of single peasants, either male or female, separate from their families; he forbade their sale in the markets; and no one could purchase or own serfs unless he had at the same time twenty acres of land for each family. But all these tutelary laws were more or less evaded during his reign. He permitted the nobles freely to emancipate their serfs; but very few of them followed the example set by Prince Alexander Galitzine and a few others, and not more than three hundred thousand families were thus set free. Nicholas I. also spoke favorably of emancipation, and even attempted it, but unsuccessfully.

During all this period, military service was a great engine of emancipation. Enlisted serfs were forever free, together with their wives and children. But military service lasted for twenty-five or thirty years, and was often more oppressive than serfdom in the village.

During the seventeenth and eighteenth centuries, the peasantry now and then avenged their wrongs by isolated murders of the more oppressive masters and their families. Partial insurrections even took place, the most celebrated of which is that of Pugatschoff under Catharine II., which swept over the bodies of slain nobles and officials, from the mountains of Orembourg to the very gates of Moscow.

But the day of justice now dawns upon Russia. The whole Christian world glorifies the efforts of Alexander II., supported by a considerable portion of the nobles, to restore freedom and homesteads to the twenty millions of serfs. The success of the great emancipation movement is beyond doubt, beyond even the possibility of being stopped, although the carrying out of such a colossal revolution requires time and meets with many impediments.

At the example of Russia the tributary nomads of Asiatic Tartary have emancipated their slaves and abjured further enslavement; and Turkey, likewise, has inscribed her name upon the grand roll of emancipating empires.

Thus the whole ancient world shakes off slavery, and attempts to wash away its ancient and bloody stain; while the New World, or at least a part of it, still glories in the barbarous abomination.

No special law in Poland decreed the serfdom of the rural population, nor in Russia their transformation into chattels. Nowhere, indeed, in the whole history of man has the conception of justice and law been so degraded as to legislate freemen, or those partially free, out of their sacred and inherent rights, beforehand. The most bloody records of humanity have not preserved any such act of legislation, and even the name of a Nero or a Heliogabalus are free from such a stain. It was left to the modern worshippers of the blood-reeking slave-demon to enact such laws; it was left to the highest judicial tribunal of the United States to brand into the brow of justice, there to remain for eternities, the infernal Dred Scott decision.

XXI. Conclusion

These pages do not touch on slavery among the Spaniards. Under the Roman republic and empire, Spain shared the lot of the other provinces, as Gaul, etc.; and what has been said in relation to slavery in the Roman world applies to her also. The results of the German invasions, and the establishment of the Goths in Spain, were similar in their bearings to what we have already seen as taking place in Gaul and Italy. Scarcely had the two races begun to fuse on the soil of Spain, and the relations between the conqueror and the conquered to be modified and softened, when the invasions by the Moors (whose domination lasted for nearly seven centuries), threw the Spaniards into internal wars. Their protracted efforts to expel the invaders fostered the preponderance of the men of the sword; and there is every likelihood that the unavoidable sequellæ of war contributed to preserve longer in Spain than in any of the other nationalities that arose out of the ruins of the Roman empire, certain of the features of domestic slavery, of bondage, and the feudal tenure. The final expulsion of the Moors from the Iberian peninsula was almost immediately followed by the discovery of the continent of America, and by the formation here of a great Spanish empire, and the introduction thereinto of Africans as domestic slaves. To master the various relations of property and villeinage, of bondage and chattelhood in Spain and in the Spanish Main, requires special studies, for which, indeed, we have as yet no sufficient material. At least I had none such within my reach-none that was, to my mind, conclusive and satisfactory. The Spanish republics nobly satisfied the hopes of humanity by abolishing all kinds of bondage and all distinctions of race. The Peruvian republic paid to the owners three hundred dollars per head for each slave, of every age and both sexes, and then liberated them. It may be emphatically asserted, that the protracted political confusion prevailing in the Spanish American States, has its sources not in the act of emancipatory justice, but that it is the result of altogether different causes. These, however, do not come within the compass of the present investigation.

The many analogies between domestic slavery as practised by various nations and races of the past, and as it now exists in our Slave States, have been often enough pointed out. These analogies prove beyond doubt that slavery always corrupts the slave-holder and the whole community-be the ethnic peculiarities of the enslaved race what they may.

History shows slavery to have been always most luxuriant in those nations where society was most disorganized, just as noxious animals and plants multiply in putrefaction and rottenness. Facts reveal to us how far the disorder has already penetrated Southern life; and it would progress even more rapidly were it not for the purifying and healing influences (feeble though they now be) coming from the North.

The civilized Christian world follows with ever-increasing interest the stages of the political struggle in the American Union-sympathizing deeply with those who, though they cannot hope to effect an immediate cure, yet seek to arrest the growth of the fatal disorder.[21]

Slavery is as fatal to society as are the Southern and tropical swamps to human life. And as material culture drains the marshes, clears the forests, and renders the soil productive and the air healthy: so in like manner, will moral and social culture yet make the institutions of this republic rich and refulgent-unblighted by the presence of a slave!

The source of many, if not of all, the political and administrative disorders in these States, is to be found in the struggles occasioned by the arrogant and everlasting encroachments on liberty and on the Union, by the militant worshippers of slavery. To cure these disorders, the *growth* of the disease its expansion over yet uninfected territories —*must be stopped*: such must be the first step in a sanitary direction; and the paramount duty of self-preservation now commands its adoption. This whole question of Slavery, too, must be forced back to where it was left by the immortal expounders of Southern instinct and intuition on slavery, those noble patriots-Henry, Laurens, Washington, Jefferson, Mason, Randolph, and a host of other great names-now forsworn by their political descendants. To conceal the vulture that is devouring their vitals, the fanatical upholders of slavery pervert and degrade all that humanity, morality, civilization and history have recognized as sacred.

The slave-orators and so-called statesmen avouch "that no one in the South believes in popular sovereignty." This unbelief is natural enough; for popular sovereignty can only exist in intelligent, orderly and laborious communities. It exists in the Free States, and here freemen practically believe in and uphold it. But an ignorant and degraded population of oligarchs, oppressors and slave-breeders never were capable of exercising popular sovereignty, and consequently nowhere could they ever have faith in it: barbarians generally mistrust civilization. Universal suffrage is *not* a failure in the villages and townships of the Free States, though it does fail on slave plantations, or among a so-called free population drilled and led by oligarchs.

Human institutions experience ups and downs-they have their luminous and their gloomy epochs. Ignorant and debased masses throw a shadow over universal suffrage and self-government; and only genuine freedom goes hand in hand with reason, knowledge and morality. These, too, mutually reproduce each other. It is, therefore, easy to be understood how freedom disappears from the Slave South, and is no more cherished or believed in.

Many consider the American institution of self-government as a new experiment; and European serviles and American slave oligarchs utter fearful forebodings that the experiment is already a failure. But the prophecy only expresses their desires. For this so-called experiment is but the natural, progressive development of man, and for this reason proves itself every day more and more successful in the Free States. The kingdoms and nations of the old world are now diligently studying this experiment of freedom, and trying to appropriate its beneficent results. Agents of European governments uninterruptedly investigate the system of free communal schools, the manufactures, the inventions, the multifarious industrial and agricultural progress of the Free States. But no government sends its messengers to study out the condition of slave plantations, slave huts, or slave pens; for they know well that by the action of self-government and universal suffrage, qualitative and quantitative knowledge is more generally spread, and has reached a far higher grade in the American Free States than among all the militant oligarchs and knight-errants of slavery the world over.

An experiment generally proves successful if made with properly adapted and unadulterated materials. A structure raised on a treacherous foundation and built with rotten materials must fall. It is an experiment altogether new to the human race to construct a society and government with chattelhood as an integral element. It is an experiment to attempt to bring down horrified humanity on its knees to the worship of chattelhood and the devilish slave traffic. Such an experiment is now being tried by the apostles of slavery; and that too, though morality, civilization and history have unanimously and forever pronounced the sentence of condemnation against holding property in man. The civilized and Christian world of both hemispheres and every race unanimously awarded to JOHN BROWN the crown of a martyr, who fell in the cause of human liberty.

One deviation from a sound social principle is speedily followed by another; violence ever begets violence; and this is the fatal genesis of all oppressions and tyrannies. The oligarchic despotism in the Slave States runs rapidly through all the stages with which individual despotism has filled the dark records of history. It has already succeeded in the suppression of free speech and even free thought, violation of seal, censorship of the press, and the centring of political control in the hands of officials and lacqueys. If individual tyrants dispatch their victims by special executioners, lynch law and mob law-although often executed by misguided "poor whites" —are as lawless as the murders of the tyrant, and bear a striking analogy to the executions perpetrated by agents or court-martials. Despotism drills the masses in all kinds of degradation: thus a part of the population of the Slave States is drilled in ignorance by the slaveholders, and blindly perpetrate their murderous biddings. To these deluded men who execute the bloody behests of the tyrant, the words of the Christ on Calvary apply: "Forgive them; *for they know not what they do.*"

A society based on a violation of cardinal human rights can never be considered free. Freemen are never governed by violent passions. Injustice and tyranny cannot recede; they divorce themselves from mercy, and are guilty of the most remorseless actions: thus fatally, of late, the gallows was once more ennobled. Executions and burning at the stake, amid the applaudings of the ignorant and the infuriated, are nothing new in history; and neither is the transmission of the names of the murderers to the maledictions of eternity.

Human society will perhaps always be subject, in one shape or another, to wrongs and disorders: but humanity specially revolts at the hideous wrongs which now exist, such as the claim of property in man, and the traffic in man. As long as this claim is found on the legal record, as long as slavery exists as a common fact, futile will be all efforts to stifle the voice of freedom, to crush into oblivion the question of slavery, or to expel it from the chambers of legislation or the tribunals of the people. It will and must ever reappear on the surface: —as in bodily disorders, when the virus has eaten its way into the innermost organism, external eruptions may be locally, healed or closed up, but again they reappear on another spot, or attack another organ, until a radical cure relieves the body from the poison. Until utterly destroyed, slavery will always be paramount to all other political questions, to all political complications, and it will forever force its way into them all. To a greater or less degree, diseases assume the characteristics of a prevailing epidemic. When several diseases are complicated together, the physician first attempts to cure the most virulent and dangerous. This question of slavery must have a solution; and it is in vain that the weak-minded deny the existence of the devouring disorder, or attempt to conjure it with paltry expedients.

Humanity would gratefully applaud even an intermediate step from absolute chattelhood toward emancipation, or any public measure foreshadowing an intention on the part of the slave-holding States to become humane. First of all, let them recognize in the bondman the sacred, imprescriptible, natural rights of man and of family; then let them abandon the slave traffic, and thus avoid separation of man and wife, of parent and child. Even the transformation of the slaves into serfs, into *adscripti glebæ*, would be an alleviation, and a cheering sign of progress. Certainly, there are economic impediments which stand in the way of immediate and absolute emancipation. The emancipated might be interested in labor, in the soil, and in freedom, by the possession of homesteads, even if they remained under the control of their masters. The noble examples set by Prussia and Russia in Europe, and by England in her West Indian possessions, might be modified and adapted to circumstances and to special conditions. But the present extollers of human bondage never will listen to the imploring voice of humanity, or to the admonishing warnings of history; they deliberately prepare volcanic eruptions for coming generations.

Pro-slavery orators sometimes grow florid, sentimental, and idyllic in their praises and glorification of slavery. But gaseous speeches emanate not from vigorous or healthy minds. Gas generally arises from substances in process of decomposition. Posterity venerates only the names of the orators who stand up for a sacred cause or a grand idea, who act under generous impulses, who defend human rights and liberties, and who brand with infamy every kind of oppression.

Every day freedom gets a firmer and more enduring foothold in Europe. Every nation of the old continent enjoys greater liberty to-day than it did on the birthday of the American Republic. The disorders which are the accumulation of almost countless centuries, slowly, but nevertheless uninterruptedly, melt away before the breath of the ever-vigorous spirit of humanity. After a protracted experience of sufferings, old Europe, centuries ago, got rid of domestic slavery.

But what civilization and humanity assert to be their greatest afflictions are upheld as blessings in this New World by the Young Republic. Sadness and even despair fill the mind when witnessing the loftiest and best social structure ever erected by man sapped to its foundations by the sacrilegious champions of human bondage!

Footnotes

1.   A Manual of Pathological Anatomy, by Carl Rokitansky, M.D. Translated from the German, by Edward Swaine, M.D., Fellow of the Royal College of Physicians.

2.   "America and Europe," chap. X.

3.   Among the neutral publications on American slavery, the most remarkable and instructive is the work entitled "The Law of Freedom and Bondage in the United States," by John Codman Hurt.

4.   The term *Japhetic* is rather confused and unscientific. It is used here as being more popularly intelligible.

5.   Herodotus.

6.   The name *Carthage* signifies a "new borough," or "city."

7.   The old colonial customs and legal regulations in America, fully confirm the above statements. *White* servants, with or without indenture, were kept in bondage by their masters, as were other chattels, and sometimes, though rarely, these servants were even sold. Without, therefore, going back to any European origin, it may be peremptorily asserted that it is comparatively a short time since the sires of many haughty militant slavery defenders were bondsmen on American soil.

8.   Flavius Josephus says, that under the Herods, Judea contained double the population established by the census of David. Perhaps this account is exaggerated; but, at any rate, it shows a great and positive increase.

9.   In contradistinction to Aryanized Shemites or Chaldeans, known as Assyrians and Babylonians of the second epoch, and modern Kurdes. Ethnology and comparative philology everywhere discover similar bifurcations almost at the sources of ethnic life. These bifurcations are explained by natural growth and by the fusion of various tribes and nations. Thus Baktrya, Persia and Media present us with Aryas and Indo-Scythes or Aryanized Tartars. So, too, all primitive races divide and subdivide in the same manner within themselves. The Shemites divided into Chaldeans and Canaanites, and then into Arabs, Hebrews, etc. The Aryas divided first into two groups-the eastern, from which, in turn, sprang the Zend and Sanscrit-speaking Aryas or Iranians and Hindus-and the western group, ancestors of the various European races. Of these latter, one branch immigrated into Greece and Italy, there giving rise again to Ionians and Dorians, Italiots and Latins, and the Greek and Latin languages; while another formed the Gaels or Gadheals and Kimri, the Gadhealic and the Brizonec being the principal dialects. Then we have their offshoots-as Belgæ, Kimbro-Belgæ, Finnic-Belgæ, etc. So also the Slavic stem, split into Serb, Wendish, etc.

10.   The philological analysis of the arrow-headed characters and inscriptions discovered in the ruins of Nineveh (Khorsabad) and of Babylon, and on various other spots of the ancient Persian empire, give us some idea of the various ethnic elements which composed the Assyrian and Babylonian empires. Probability, founded on comparative philology, attributes the invention of the arrow-headed characters to a Tartar (Scythic) people or race. Transmitted, in all likelihood, from people to people; increased, fused in usage and application by various languages and dialects, these cuneiform characters-as used for Assyrian, Babylonian and Persian inscriptions-are now ethnically and philologically classified into two main divisions-the Anaryan and the Aryan. The Aryan comprises the Old Persian; the Anaryan of the Ninevite relics is the result of thirteen ethnic

and philologic combinations, and was used by the five following peoples, all known to history. 1. Medo-Scythians; 2. Casdo-Scythians; 3. Susians; 4. Ancient Armenians; 5. Assyrians. The following are the thirteen combinations: 1. Pure hieroglyphs; 2. Hieratic signs-neither yet arrow-headed; 3. Old Scythic or Tartar arrow-heads; 4. New Tartar (new under Assyria); 5. Old Susian; 6. New Susian; 7. Old Armenian; 8. New Armenian; 9. Old Assyrian; 10. New Assyrian; 11. Old Babylonian; 12. New Babylonian; 13. Demotic Babylonian. —*Oppert.*

11. The Sanscrit has about one hundred and forty appellations for the "horse" (mare and colt included); and comparative philology demonstrates their primitive roots to be preserved in almost all European languages.

12. Edward A. Pollard, letter to the *Tribune.*

13. So the poor whites of the South emigrate and settle in the Western territories, and the planters magnify their plantations and their chattels.

14. The Cæsars proper end with Nero, and then begin the emperors of various families and even nationalities.

15. See speech of Senator Mason of Virginia.

16. So to-day no law creates or gives a definition of "sand-hillers," "clay-eaters," and other brutalized poor whites in the South, who are rapidly approaching slavery.

17. See "America and Europe," by the present writer.

18. Romans as citizens of the empire and not of the city of Rome.

19. Certain pro-slavery organs and small yelpers (see "Southern Wealth," etc., New York, 1860) defame the memory of the Henries and Elizabeths for their generous action toward the serfs, forgetting that such royal decrees, in many cases, *liberated their own direct ancestors.*

20. The name of *slave* in the Slavi language, is derived either from *slava*, "renown," or from *slowo*, "the verb." It is supposed that the Slavi called themselves thus as having the gift of speech, of *the verb*, in contradistinction to those speaking an unintelligible language, whom they called *niemy*, "mute," wherefrom *nemets*, "a German."

21. What in common politics is called a "party," "an expedient," never had even the slightest influence upon my convictions or action-events having furnished me more than one occasion to sacrifice to principle some leaves of my existence. I now use my right of American citizenship in voting the "Republican" ticket, the tendencies and actions of that organization satisfying my convictions. But excepting some few personal friends, the leaders of the party, whether in this city, the State, or the Union, are scarcely known to me even by name.

Made in the USA
Monee, IL
08 December 2024

72793309R00059